CISTERCIAN STUDIES SERIES: NUMBER FIFTY-ONE

IN QUEST OF THE ABSOLUTE

CISTERCIAN STUDIES SERIES: NUMBER FIFTY-ONE

IN QUEST OF THE ABSOLUTE:
THE LIFE AND WORK OF
JULES MONCHANIN

edited and translated by

J. G. Weber

Kalamazoo: Cistercian Publications, Inc.
London: A. R. Mowbray & Co Ltd.
1977

CISTERCIAN STUDIES SERIES

Permission to publish this volume has been received from
Paul V. Donovan, Bishop of Kalamazoo.

Copyright, translation, Cistercian Publications, Inc. 1976
French, as noted: Editions du Centurion, Paris Casterman s.a. éditeurs,
Tournai-Paris

Library of Congress Cataloging in Publication Data

Monchanin, Jules.
    In quest of the absolute.

    (Cistercian studies series; no. 51)
    Bibliography: p.
    1. Monchanin, Jules. 2. Catholics in India—Biography. 3. Theology—
Addresses, essays, lectures. I. Weber, Joseph, 1931- II. Title. III. Series.
BX4705. M6312A34   282'.092'4 [B]   77-3596
ISBN 0-87907-851-0

Cistercian Publications, Inc.
1749 West Michigan Avenue - WMU
Kalamazoo, Michigan 49008

ISBN (case) 0 87907 851 0
(paper) 0 87907 951 7

A. R. Mowbray & Co Ltd
Saint Thomas House
Becket Street
Oxford OX1 1SJ

ISBN (paper) 0 264 66474 0

Typeset at the Cloister Printery; New Riegel, Ohio 44853

EDITOR'S NOTE

These texts have been drawn and edited in large part from the selection of Jules Monchanin's writings presented by his friend Edouard Duperray (Jules Monchanin. *Ecrits spirituels*. Paris: Centurion, 1965) as well as a number of other writings by Monchanin.

Grateful acknowledgement is made to my wife, to Henri de Lubac *sj*, † Henri Le Saux *osb*, Edouard Duperray, Dr Raymond Panikkar, and Miss Pheme Perkins for their help and encouragement in the preparation of this book.

PUBLISHER'S NOTE

Cistercian Publications expresses its gratitude to Fr Bede Griffiths for his encouragement in the publication of this volume, and to Editions du Centurion and to Casterman s.a. éditeurs, publishers of the French language editions of Fr Monchanin's works and biography, who have graciously permitted us to use translations of materials under their copyright.

Shanti Vanam, Easter 1957

PREFACE

'Will I someday know the same joy,' wrote Jules Monchanin of a similar venture in China, 'that in India too—from its soil and spirit—there will come a monastic life dedicated to contemplation?' When Monchanin died in 1957, the monastic life of which he had dreamed and which had begun to take shape in the little *ashram* which he had founded at *Shantivanam* had still hardly taken root. But he had planted a seed which was destined to grow and the influence of his life and thought has continued to spread. In France his memory has always been cherished by a small group of friends, and the book of his friend Henri de Lubac, *Images de l'Abbé Monchanin,* has made him known to a wider circle. The fact that so many years after his death an account of his life and work should be written in America shows that his importance is not confined to France. In India also, though his name is still not well-known, his influence has continued to grow. His ideal of a monastic life which should be 'totally Indian and totally Christian' is now accepted by the Church as a whole—as was shown in the National Seminar in Bangalore in 1969. If his dream is still slow of realisation, this is perhaps because he saw so far and his thought went so deep. He himself had no illusions about the success of his work. 'I must be buried in this land of India,'

1

he wrote, 'somewhat like de Foucauld in the land of the Sahara, to be sanctified by it and to make it fertile.'

The comparison with Charles de Foucauld is significant. Like de Foucauld, he did not live to see a community grow up round him. He was willing to die that life might come up after him. Like de Foucauld, Monchanin was a contemplative, and he knew that the contemplative life can only come through death and resurrection. 'I feel and know,' he wrote, 'that the more I disappear as an individual, the more the Spirit will work his way with this India, which he wishes to engulf in unfathomable contemplation.' This was the vision which sustained him through all the difficulties and the deep frustration of his life, so that he could accept them not only with resignation but with joy. His desire was that 'what is deepest in Christianity may be grafted onto what is deepest in India'. This he knew can only be a work of time and patience. It remains still an ideal to be realised, but there are signs today that an awakening to this ideal is taking place in the Church in India. Young Indians are beginning to discover the depth of their own Indian tradition and also the depth of Christianity. 'Our *Advaita* and the praise of the Trinity are our only aim,' wrote Monchanin, and with these words he put his finger on the precise point where the meeting in depth between Indian and the Christian faith has to take place.

The Hindu experience of the *Atman*, the ground alike of being and of consciousness as 'one without a second', and the Christian experience of God as a Trinity of Persons, are complementary truths. Within the depths of the One there is revealed a communion of knowledge and love, which does not destroy but perfects the unity of the One Being. But to discover this point of unity in the two traditions we have to ascend, as Monchanin observed, to the source of both traditions, to the point at which they originally burst forth and took shape, before they had hardened into systems. This was the task he had set himself: 'to rethink everything in the light of theology, and to rethink theology through mysticism', as his friend Père de Lubac had put it to him. This task remains still to be fulfilled, but again there are others who are now following the same path. The idea is growing that it is only in an *ashram*, where the conditions are present for a life of contemplation, that an Indian Christian theology can come into being. It was Monchanin's vocation not to reach the goal to which he aspired, but to open the way to it for others. The *ashram* which he founded remains as a witness to the ideal of a contemplative life which he had set before him, and his life and writings remain to inspire others with the vision of a Christian contemplation which shall have assimilated the wisdom of India, and a theology in which the genius of India shall find expression in Christian terms.

Apart from a memoir translation of some of his writings in English which is now out of print, this is the first account of Monchanin's life and work in English. Monchanin was many years ahead of his time, and perhaps it is only now that the full significance of his life and work for India and the world can be realised. A friend of the Abbé Couturier and of Père de Lubac, he anticipated many of the ideas of ecumenism and of the new theology which came to light in the second Vatican Council, and he was one of the first to appreciate the work of Teilhard de Chardin. It is with these great leaders of thought in modern times that he belongs. It is to be hoped that his life and thought will now become known to a wider circle of English-speaking people.

Bede Griffiths

Shantivanam
Kulitalai
South India

CONTENTS

INTRODUCTION*

O N 5 MAY 1939, after many years of patient waiting, Jules Monchanin set out from Marseilles for India. had attempted for some ten years to secure the approval of an Indian bishop for a plan of total adaptation to Indian life, and, although two bishops were interested by the originality and uniqueness of Monchanin's plan of a Christian-Hindu contemplative life, at once totally Christian and full Hindu, each for his own reason was hesitant to have the French priest establish a foundation in his diocese. But Monchanin did finally receive the approval of Bishop Mendonça of Tiruchirapalli, South India, who at first assigned him to a parish ministry principally among widely scattered and isolated Christian families in village communities. For a decade he was to serve in this way, still very far from his goal. They were years of great physical hardship and profound loneliness, years of preparation for a contemplative life he sometimes doubted would be realized.

Finally in 1950, with Henri Le Saux, a French Benedictine, who had been seeking a similar way of life and who now joined him, Monchanin founded at Kulitalai along the bank of the Kavery River an *ashram*, a hermitage dedicated to the adoration of the Trinity. They called the *ashram Saccidānanda:* Sat (Being), Cit (Logos), Ananda (Bliss of

Love and Beauty). The goal was to form the first nucleus of a monastery. It would be, more exactly, a *laura*, a grouping of neighboring hermitages, like the laura of Saint Sabas in ancient Palestine. Life would be totally Indian, totally Christian: a Benedictine *ashram*, with meditative reading of the Vedas and the Bible, a simple vegetarian diet, straw mats for sitting and sleeping, and the wearing of the *kavi* of the Hindu holy man. Monchanin's hope was to 'crystallize and transubstantiate the search of the Hindu *sannyāsi*'. 'Advaita [non-dualism] and the praise of the Trinity,' he said, 'are our only aim. This means that we must grasp the authentic Hindu search for God in order to Christianize it, starting with ourselves first of all, from within.'

Monchanin had an extraordinary vision of mankind and the nature of religion—in both the Hindu and Christian traditions. He was dissatisfied with the idea of setting up in the East what might be called bastions of Western Christianity, which often became enclaves of Christian colonialism or at best cultural anomalies. He sought, rather, to recover the common spiritual experience of Christianity and Hinduism. This common ground, a contemplative one, is found at the moment they are closest to their origin, when they still possess what might be called their original explosive energy. The true union of Christianity and Hinduism is to be sought in their earliest sources. For Hinduism this is the time between the Brahmanas and Buddhism, and for Christianity it means the time before the patristic synthesis of the fifth century, when Christianity was swept up into Mediterranean civilization. In its radical and universal scope, Monchanin's quest and synthesis of Hindu and Western religious and philosophical thought can be compared to Teilhard's paleontological discoveries in China and his synthesis of science and Western spirituality.

There was little in his family life, his schooling, his early years, that would have pointed to this radical reorientation.

Monchanin was born in France on 10 April 1895, in a small town in the Beaujolais region not far from Lyons, and at a rather early age he decided to become a priest. In 1922, when he completed his theological studies at the Major Seminary at Francheville, he was ordained for the diocese of Lyons. His seminary professors had recognized in him unusual intellectual gifts and consequently had urged him to continue his studies toward the doctorate in theology. For a time Monchanin did so, and he received a licentiate in theology. His teachers were some of the same theologians who influenced his friend Henri de Lubac and Pierre Teilhard de Chardin: Tixeront, Podechard, Jacquier, Valensin. It was Valensin, too, who acted as his sponsor for the *Société lyonnaise de philosophie*.

But Monchanin decided against continuing his formal theological studies and asked the archbishop for reassignment to a miners' parish in one of the suburbs of Lyons. He served there for one year and subsequently in two other parishes in Lyons. In 1932, a serious illness obliged him to give up much of his active work, and for a time he was chaplain to a suburban orphanage and later to a boarding school for boys, where one of his directees was the poet, Pierre Emmanuel.

During this period when he was engaged in such varied forms of ministry, he also committed himself to an intellectual apostolate among university students and professors. He served as adviser to organizations of scientists, philosophers, and students, such as the *Cercle Saint Jean-Baptiste*, and *Groupe lyonnais d'études médicales, philosophiques, et biologiques* and the *Chronique social*. He also worked closely with other groups engaged in ecumenical and Judeo-Christian studies. In addition to this, he was pursuing advanced studies in the language and culture of the Far East, principally Sanskrit, comparative religion, and missiology.

Through his reading, Monchanin, from the time of his adolescence, had been more and more drawn to India, its people, history, and religion. But it was not until 1938 that he received the permission of his bishop to enter the *Société des Auxiliaires des Missions*, a missionary community, recently founded in Belgium by Fathers Lebbe and Boland. The apostolate of this group was directed primarily toward China, and it was Father Monchanin who sought to establish a point of Christian 'insertion' or 'grafting', as he called it, into the spiritual life of India by means of a deep and total adaptation to the contemplative life of a Hindu *sannyāsi*.

Monchanin's mission was, in human terms, a failure, and he saw this as a sign—a proof—of its ultimate fruitfulness. He was frequently reminded of Foucauld, and he often quoted the words of Christ in John 12:24-25('Unless the seed die, it cannot bear fruit abundantly.' He realized his vocation in a death uprooted from his beloved India. (Monchanin died on 10 October 1957 in Paris, where he had been sent for medical treatment.)   His death was not sterility but parturition.   The seed did take root.   A decade later, Dom Bede Griffiths and two Indian monks from Kurisumala left their own Christian *ashram* and have established themselves at Kulitalai to continue, along with Henri Le Saux, the quest for the absolute which Jules Monchanin had undertaken many years before.

Monchanin's deep love of India, the land of his vocation and the people with whom he had identified himself, made it possible for his *ashram*, his life, his prayer to over-reach time and space to become universal in dimension.   Universality was for him the law of all Christian life:

> Dilate the Church.   We each have our unique
> place. The highest parts of this Body are the most
> irreplaceable. Dilate the Church by your prayer.
> Never will it be the prayer of a person in isolation.
> It will be a prayer as open as Christ's arms on the
> cross, as vast as Redemption. You will have the
> restlessness of the world to save—constant inter-
> cession for the union of Christians. For the world
> to believe that God sent his word, his disciples
> must appear united. Restlessness of those who do
> not believe in the one Mediator, who have kept to

the belief in the God of Abraham—the restlessness of Israel, the restlessness of Islam—and of the remainder of the world: China so ready to grasp all the resonances of the Incarnation; India thirsting for contemplation; primitive peoples unaware of the obstacle we know so well, the over-analytic mind—and for that portion of humanity which has rejected God and the battle. In this way, yours prayers will be catholic, and fully so.

The following pages seek to introduce English-speaking readers to the life, the thought, and the mission of a man 'seized by the Spirit', who has pointed the way to the deepest form of spiritual union between Christianity and Hinduism.

J.G.W.

PART ONE
Life and Work

APPROACHES TO INDIA

J ULES MONCHANIN SET OUT FOR INDIA on 5 May
1939, fulfilling a hope and a desire he had had for many
years. He was going to serve in India in the diocese of a
native Indian bishop, Msgr Joseph Mendonça of Tiruchirapalli. At the age of forty-five, when most priests are firmly
established in their ministry or intellectual careers, Father
Monchanin left his native land for a new beginning, a new
life in a different culture, a culture with which he had
identified himself since early youth. Of this vocation to India
he wrote:

> I had always been drawn by India. If you look at
> the development of a vocation, you find its roots in
> the earliest years of childhood. You discern signs
> which were at first unnoticed. The same thing is
> found in mysticism. As in Heidegger's conception
> of time, it is the future which draws the present
> and the past. So there was always within me this
> attraction toward India, like a preadaptation to
> India, something congenital. At first it was
> primarily intellectual, and it had not yet taken
> shape in a definite vocation.
>
> If God hadn't willed certain encounters, my life
> would have unfolded rather dully, without devel-

13

opment, without florescence. The working out of a
person's destiny is always a great mystery. The
graces received are bound to so many others.
There are incarnate graces which make you go
from the intellectual level to the vital level.

There was little in Monchanin's earliest years which would
make one expect this vocation to India. His childhood was
marked by frequent periods of sickness, particularly attacks of
asthma, from which he was never to be free during his life.
This early experience of physical suffering was, however, not
without fruit. It allowed him to understand, in later years,
the mystery of suffering, the role of evil in the life of the
Christian and in the building up of the Mystical Body of
Christ. He was to write later:

All suffering is born of the finite. All suffering is
of self, a giving birth, generative of a higher form
of being.

Christ assumes all sorrow, cosmic sorrow. The
passion of the Mystical Body is coextensive with
humanity and with creation.

Factus peccatum pro nobis. (For our sake he
made him into sin—2 Cor 5:21). Suffering is the
reflection of cosmic sin in the sentient world. By
assuming suffering, Christ clothes himself in
sinfulness.

The very Passion is transmuted into the Resurrection, into Paschal joy, and the evil of the world
becomes the joy of the world.

The reversals which are part of human suffering
are righted to the extent that they become the
suffering of Christ (Christ's to an unlimited extent
and man's to an extent conditioned by his
adherence to Christ).

Thus through Christ the reality of suffering coincides with its essence: it is actually a parturition.

Instead of merely putting up with suffering, as is the case in every life not yet regenerated by sharing in the Paschal mystery, the Christian welcomes it, embraces it, understands it (suffering and even death itself), and he is grasped in it, grasped in the double meaning of enveloped and illuminated, *comprehendam sicut et comprehensus sum* (I shall know as fully as I am known—1 Cor 13:12). Realization of the Gospel phrases: 'Unless the seed die' and 'He who loses his life (soul) finds it'—Matt 10:39 (the *law*, in the strict sense, of the spiritual world).

Confined as he was by his health to the care of his mother and elder sister, Monchanin spent the first twelve years of his life removed from the outside world, and his taste for introspection was allowed to develop. He lived in the world of his own imagination, without contact with other children. His was a limited horizon, hardly seeming the kind that would arouse a desire to know other persons and other countries.

During his years in secondary school, he began to be interested in Indian thought through reading Sénart's work on Buddhism.[1] But the interest was merely a passing one. It was in fact much later, during the first years of his priestly ministry, that he was drawn back to his early interest in India. Counselling priests who were preparing for the missions, Father Monchanin had to reflect on those problems facing the Church in spreading the Gospel which were due to political and economic upheavals in Asia and on the conditions for the deep penetration of the Christian message into these ancient civilizations. During the same period, he met Indian students in France who opened up to him the profundity of the Hindu religious tradition. He was quick to see the immense gain that the Christianization of such a deeply spiritual land as India would be for the Church. And thus through his reading, spiritual counselling, and personal contacts, he came to realize that he was himself called by God to make the complete and humble gift of his life to the Church in India.

He became fully aware of this vocation during a serious illness in March, 1932. On the 26 of that month, Passion Sunday, his condition was so critical that he seemed very near death, and he received the last sacraments of the Church. There was only one regret that he felt in his life, that of dying outside India. He promised God that, if he were to recover, he would dedicate himself to the salvation of India.

His health was restored, and he spent all his available free time familiarizing himself with Indian culture, taking courses in Sanskrit, immersing himself in Indian philosophy, and trying, through works of art, to grasp Indian sensibility. He made friends with Indian families and used every opportunity to learn in detail from missionaries about the state of Christianity in India and the conditions of missionary life.

Endowed with an extraordinary capacity for assimilation and with a prodigious memory, he very quickly acquired a profound knowledge of Indian thought, which was recognized by the great Indologists of his time. 'Had he wished,' wrote Olivier Lacombe, 'his broad and deep theological esthetic and even philological background would have allowed him to write one or several great books on India.'[2] Jean Filliozat said of him: 'The first time that I met Father Monchanin was at a meeting of Indologists. He read a paper analyzing the then quite new theories that several authors had advanced on the supposed Dravidian origins of the civilization of the Indus. His paper and analysis were profoundly lucid and informative.'[3] The extent of his knowledge and vision in comparing Hinduism and Christianity is evidenced particularly in his articles, such as 'L'Inde et la Contemplation,'[4] or 'Yoga et Hésychasme,' and 'Apophatisme et Apavada.'[5]

His meeting and the long conversations with Msgr Peter,

the Indian bishop of Kumbakonam, strengthened his decision to leave for India. At first the bishop agreed to have Father Monchanin come to his diocese. But a few months later he was obliged, with personal disappointment, to change his mind because of certain difficulties inherent in the mission.

Monchanin was not discouraged. Toward the middle of the summer of 1935 he asked his archbishop, Cardinal Maurin, for authorization to follow his calling to the missionary life. Permission was refused, the Cardinal being reluctant to lose a member of the clergy of Lyons whose influence was felt beyond the school where Monchanin served as chaplain and even beyond the diocese itself.

During these years of waiting, Father Monchanin's apostolic activity was quite extensive. He was an active member of the *Groupe lyonnais d'études médicales, philosophiques et biologiques*, theological adviser to the *Section médicale et biologique du Secrétariat social* directed by Doctor René Biot, and he was also spiritual adviser to a Paris group pursuing Judeo-Christian studies. He participated regularly in ecumenical meetings organized between Catholic and Protestant theologians by Father Couturier and in study groups bringing together Marxists and Christians. He was among the early supporters of the review *Esprit*, edited by Emmanuel Mounier. He continued to follow Mounier's work very closely, and later when Mounier died in 1950, he presented a magnificent description of him in a lecture read at Pondicherry. Often sought after as a lecturer, he frequently addressed groups of artists, painters, and musicians, never refusing an invitation to speak where he thought he could bear witness to his faith and intellectual charity. But it was to spiritual work that he gave priority, preaching retreats to students, to different sodalities and missionary groups (particularly those supporting religious foundations in Islam), devoting most of his time to private spiritual counselling. The great number and variety of tributes that were written after Monchanin's death reveal the very deep influence that he had on everyone who met him.[6] In the evenings he visited the

poor in the outskirts of Lyons. Then later when he returned
to his room, taking time from his sleep, he would deepen his
knowledge of India, meditate and think.

Each year he renewed his request for permission to go to
India, and finally from Cardinal Gerlier, the new archbishop,
he received permission to enter the *Société des auxiliaires des
missions*, an order founded in Belgium by Fathers Lebbe and
Boland. The primary motivation for his entry into this
missionary society was· a desire to serve autochthonous
bishops. He had thought a great deal about the conditions
for a true implantation of the Church in non-European
civilizations. His study of the origins of Christianity had
shown him that Christianity had spread through the West,
not through the action of missionaries but through bishops.
The propagation of the Church was, he found, as Msgr
Batiffol noted, a 'multiplication of churches analogous to the
proliferation of cells.'[7]   But for the Church not to appear
foreign, for it to be truly indigenous, it must be present not
only with its dogmas, its sacraments, and institutions, but it
must also have an autochthonous hierarchy. Having an autochthonous hierarchy absolutely conditions the Chruch's
growth and work of salvation. In regard to the missionary
apostolate, serving autochthronous bishops seemed, indeed, a
prime necessity. Assignment in such a diocese seemed to him
to fulfill the conditions of humble service, of reparation for
the deficiencies of the white race, and of natural brotherhood
with the people toward whom the Spirit of God was sending
him. It was somewhat later that he wrote the following to his
future bishop:

> I hope to share the same conditions of life as
> my brothers in the priesthood in India, and always
> in the most humble place. As much as possible
> I want to become Indian, to feel and suffer like
> them, to think according to the traditional
> categories of their civilization, to pray with them,
> and to work together so that the Church will take
> root.

In October, 1938, Father Monchanin travelled to Louvain to the headquarters of the *Société des Auxiliaires des Missions*. For several months he had to remain there waiting for assignment to an Indian diocese. But up to that time the order, which had been founded in 1926 shortly after the creation of the first Chinese bishops, had not yet attempted to go beyond the borders of China. His goal of serving autochthonous bishops implied incorporation into a diocese by the person of the bishop, and his spirituality seemed to be summed up by the motto that Father Lebbe had inscribed at the entrance to his two monasteries:[8] total renunciation, perfect charity, constant joy—emphasizing total, perfect, and constant. But such an ideal appeared at that time illusory and unrealizable. The Chinese bishops themselves showed a certain hesitancy and considered that the project could only be an 'experiment.'

In India, the matter had not been discussed before Father Monchanin's earlier meeting with the Bishop of Kumbakonam. As the bishop had been unable to receive him into his diocese, it was necessary for him to find another way of entering India. On the advice of Father Hublou sj, chaplain of AUCAM,[9] Father Monchanin wrote to Father Kalathil, an Indian Jesuit in Tiruchirapalli, for his personal help. Tiruchirapalli seemed preferable to Calcutta, which was the city that he had first considered. There, a group of Christian *Brahmans** had begun to regret the fact they had let themselves be de-Indianized by missionaries. Father Hublou suggested to Monchanin that he spend a year in their Jesuit school learning Tamil and English. This would give him time to study the situation and to become oriented before undertaking any official duties. Also at the school were some Indian Jesuits who for some time had wanted to live in the Indian fashion, a more solitary and more austere way of life. It now seemed the appropriate time.

As it would take a while to receive official approval,

---

* Indian terms are defined in the *Glossary*, pp. 185-190

Monchanin prepared for an extended stay. These last months
he spent in Belgium were marked by constant preparation for
his mission. Through his correspondence, his work, and
personal notes, we can see the growing awareness he had of
his ultimate vocation.

> There is not much to tell about my life. Things
> are going along quietly. It has been typically fall
> weather, mild, warm days followed by a nasty
> wind with heavy rain, and the last leaves are dis-
> appearing from the trees. The light is often very
> soft and there are flocks of large white birds that
> fly overhead. I don't go out much, as there is
> nothing to see (except for a beautiful painting by
> Quentin Metsys at the Church of Saint Pierre).
> Other than spending time with the Jesuits and
> sometimes Father Lamotte, a specialist in Budd-
> hism, I have little to do. I read a great deal and
> work a little. I think, and pray and I wait.

He was soon widely sought after as a lecturer. At Louvain
he spoke on 'India and the Christian Mystery' and on the
'Hymns of the Vedas.' At Brussels he spoke on 'Buddhism'
and the 'Christianization of Civilizations,' and also to the
group *Art et Louange*, on the 'Spirituality of the Artist,' from
which emerged a common desire:

> To build a chapel to Blessed John Ruysbroeck
> in the forest of Groenendael, a place of pilgrimage.
> (This name has always reminded me of Ruys-
> broeck.) Nothing more is left of the abbey, except
> perhaps a few stones from the foundation. But the
> site is primitive—a forest and a string of lakes. His
> tree of illumination and contemplation is there. I
> prayed to him for the order of the Trinity in India.

He also preached retreats, one three-day retreat in Brussels
at the *Auxilium*, where he spoke on 'Missionary Life and the

Trinity', talking for a total of ten hours in one day, and another for the *Auxiliaires Féminines Internationales,* where he spoke on the missions.

On the third Sunday of Advent, at Baneux, the site of the apparitions of Our Lady of the Poor, he prepared some of his order's seminary students for the diaconate. And later he visited the Trappist Monastery of Chimay, where the Abbot, who was thinking of beginning an Indian foundation, asked him to speak to his monks.

> I spoke for an hour and a half on the religious philosophies of India, and also talked at some length with the Abbot and the Master of Novices and another monk who was a professor of philosophy. The Abbot wondered, since they were seeking total adaptation to Indian life, whether they wouldn't end up one day, through lack of understanding on the part of their European brothers, being separated from the rest of the order. I think it is possible and even more than possible. India itself will have to create its own forms—for men and women—of the contemplative life.

At Christmas he stayed with the Benedictines at Lophen-les-Bruges, where in the library he found the life of Dom Joliet.

> I am reading the life of Dom Joliet who, as a naval officer in China, decided to become a Benedictine monk to convert China through monasticism. He made his monastic profession in 1897 and didn't manage to fulfill his dream until 1927. Thirty years of waiting without failing even for one day to think of it and to pray for it. So he founded his monastery and directed it for four years, and then, as it was his long-standing and strong desire to die in solitude, he became a hermit and died soon after, at the age of 65, in the joy of consummation.

> Will I someday know the same joy, that in India
> too—from its soil and its spirit—there will come a
> monastic life dedicated to contemplation? And will
> I also know the joy of being a monk there? I leave
> that to God.

His apostolic activities, his reading and his personal
encounters, far from diverting him from his vocation to India,
constantly led him back to it. He wrote openly about it to his
mother. She was the person in whom he confided the most,
and writing her about his plans was a way of preparing her
for a very painful separation.

> I do not doubt my vocation. It was recognized by
> the late Pope.[10] And I have an inner certainty
> which is much deeper—although much more
> painful—than my earlier vocation to the priest-
> hood. I am sure that my priesthood has come
> about solely—or at least principally—for my
> mission. The good that I have been able to do
> here comes from the fact that I have known from
> the beginning that God calls me to him, through
> India and many sacrifices which I cannot yet
> measure.

> Mother M.J. *ocd* told me almost from her very
> first words: 'You are called, you have a mission.'
> But this is only an echo of an inner voice which is
> stronger than anything else and one that I cannot
> resist.

> I think the essential point of my mission to India
> will be to create a contemplative life. I am
> tempted by the idea—the hope—of an Indian
> monastery of men and women. The Trappists will
> be the transition. I would like the initiative to
> come from an Indian priest, and myself to be only
> a simple monk among them. I am seeking prayers
> everywhere for that. And everywhere the reply is
> more generous than I could have expected.

Mother, you are sharing in the pain of this departure, these sufferings and this hope. Much love is asked of you, a new parturition of your son whom you love more than yourself. You won't refuse.

Last night I dreamed of the garden at Chaffangeons [11]—and the spacious grounds I knew as a child. I remember with such fondness the tree where, when I was only five years old, I so relished silence. It was there without knowing it that I learned to think and to meditate.

The first months of 1939 passed without bringing the hoped-for reply from India. There were weeks of anxious waiting during which Monchanin saw more clearly the sacrifices which would be asked of him, the harsh separation from so many dear friends, from intellectual pursuits, and from humanistic values to which he was attached. Private notes allow us to glimpse the feelings, occasionally contradictory, that he experienced as the time for his departure for India drew nearer:

I want to make myself as small as a seed in the springtime—carried by the wind of the Spirit. If only India will receive me with all my weaknesses and purify me, crucify me, and exalt God. (13 February 1939)

Is it better in some way to force God, putting myself first of all in an active night (refusing all consolation and rejecting all clear apprehension), or is it better to wait (making myself as transparent as possible)? I have always thought that one must not force God, that it is a satanic sin. But suppose God wants to be taken by violence (*violenti rapiunt illud*) by a love which sacrifices everything which is not him? I have perhaps been lacking in violence in my hunger for

God! And perhaps I have deprived many persons
of this harshness—of this heroism—in renunciation. I am facing a great self-questioning: haven't
I sinned by an excess of humanism?

In India, in any case, I intend to belong only to
God—and through nothing—to him and in him. (17
February 1939)

Pray that I don't hinder God! Several people have
told me recently that they have felt God through
me as never before in their lives. That frightens
me. (21 March 1939)

At last the long-awaited reply came. On Passion Sunday,
26 March, the seventh anniversary of the promise he had
made to dedicate himself to India, the day of the Passion of
El Hallaj, the great Muslim mystic, the following letter
arrived from Father Kalathil. 'Msgr. Mendonça, to whom I
explained your desire, is wholly enthusiastic about it and will
gladly welcome you into his diocese. I like your idea of an
apostolate with a complete adaptation to Indian life, and of a
life of prayer and study. I consulted several of our
missionary fathers. They all approve your plan.'

The next day he celebrated a Mass of thanksgiving and
made the following observations:

I do not know where I am or who I am, so much
sorrow and joy are struggling within me. Yet
underneath it all there is a kind of essential joy. I
know more than ever that God waits for me.

After a trip to Holland and a brief stay in Paris, he
returned to Lyon to bid farewell to his friends and to make
the final preparations for his departure. Concerning the long
wait that he had experienced, he wrote:

When I look back, it is impossible to regret leaving
after such a long delay. I think that it was exactly
at the moment it had to be.

In Lyons he revisited familiar places and met with friends who deeply shared many of his thoughts.

> I saw Father de Lubac again, alone and for a long time. Once more he expressed his friendship for me, saying that I would fulfill the intuition that he had had from his seminary days: to rethink everything in the light of theology and to rethink theology through mysticism, freeing it from everything incidental and regaining, through spirituality alone, everything essential. He particularly liked my notes on love and on India. He believes that it is in coming into contact with India that I will be able to rework theology much better than by going into theological problems in themselves.

On 5 May 1939 in Marseilles he boarded an English boat destined for Bombay; a trip of more than a fortnight through the Mediterranean, the Red Sea and the Indian Ocean—one of the most beautiful ocean routes in the world. The sadness he felt thinking about all that he was leaving behind was somewhat lessened by the keen interest he experienced in visiting the cradle of so many ancient civilizations. In letters addressed to family or friends he told of his thoughts as he visited different places and different civilizations.

To Edouard Duperray, Near Port-Said, 7 May 1939

> My first night was spent overwhelmed by sleep (I was so tired!): the fragrance of the red roses sent by Alice Kohn and the obsessive thought (in my dreams) that *venit hora mea.* My hour has come and it will be what God wants. I know only that I am leaving everything behind me, everything that I know, everything that I love...and that I see...far beyond....

> What will India be like? I am reading the Gospels and Rāmānuja (Lacombe's short thesis, the translation of the great Vedantic doctor).[12]

To his mother, at Sea, 8 May 1939

I think a great deal about your suffering, which is all the more painful because it is silent, without tears. I admire your strength so much. God be with you! God asks for things which cause much pain. I am beginning to feel the solitude. What will it be like later? But it had to be. The call was irresistable. With God all has to be risked without counting the cost. It is for India that I want to love beyond myself.

To Edouard Duperray from the Red Sea
Saturday, 13 May 1939.

This splendid journey goes on in brilliant light. I was able to say my Mass (the last one in Africa) in the church of the Italian Franciscans at Port-Said. I remembered everyone I love in Africa. Behind Africa, the two twin communities. I missed Damietta. Then Sinai, the barren chain with two summits: Horeb and Djebel Moussa. Both sides of the canal are desert. One of the most beautiful things was the sunset on the blue-gray sea, lengthened across an endless shore of yellow-white sand. Elsewhere, empty rocks. It looks like Tugurt—the same silence. How clearly Islam is present to me in all this. The Red Sea is very calm, so broad that you can hardly make out the coastline. We are nearer the Arabian Peninsula. I read and meditate. I am rereading Massignon and El Hallaj. On one shore is Islam and on the other memories of the Bible that Islam has covered over as well—or rather on both shores. Tomorrow we will be in Aden, 'the land of Cain'. Time goes too quickly. If you only knew how beautiful the stars are on the Red Sea, the sea 'that one crosses only once.' Until I reach the Indian Ocean, I won't be able to be free of Islam, which obsesses me more than ever.

Christ is close, too. It seems that the Church is dilating with the sliding movement of this boat, peaceful as a flight of doves.

To Edouard Duperray from the Indian Ocean
Vigil of the Ascension

Aden, cluster of blackish rocks and the crater of an extinct volcano—but not very high. No greenery except for a wretched looking shrub garden along the sea. I said Mass (the first in Asia) in a rather handsome Church. The server was an Indian and there was also a very handsome Abyssinian. Mixture of peoples. A Negro village extending the Arab village. There are Parsis, Jews, Somalis, Indians, Arabs, and most of all goats, everywhere. Impression still of Islam but a negrified Islam.

And in one day, on the feast of the Ascension I will see my chosen land.

To his mother, 16 May 1939

In two days it will be your wedding anniversary and the day of my arrival in the land that God has destined for me from all eternity. The sea is just so beautiful and calm—as smooth as glass since Marseilles.

I am full of anguish and at the same time exaltation in face of the unknown which waits for me. I know only one thing (it is a conviction which is deep within me): God does not want me anywhere else but there. I must be buried in this land of India—somewhat like Father de Foucauld in the land of the Sahara—to be sanctified and to make it fertile. Reread with me Saint John's Gospel (Ch. XIV-XVI) and the last public prayer of Jesus, so full of universalism. India and all continents are contained in it.

On Ascension Day, he disembarked at Bombay and he remained there some three days. He was disappointed by the city because of its lack of style. From there he travelled with friends to the State of Nizam to visit the grottos of Ajanta and Ellora. He particularly admired the serene beauty of the sculptures at Ajanta; and he came away from Ellora with the unforgettable memory that all India is present there—Buddhist, Jain, and Hindu. It was there, too, that he experienced for the first time the numinous quality which radiates from the temples of Southern India and which is characteristic of the great architecture of the Far East.

Trichinopoly (now called Tiruchirapalli) is a city of about 120,000 inhabitants and is located in the delta of the Kavery River. Overlooking the river is a large granite coupola. During the Pallava dynasty (7-8th century) grottos were hollowed out of the coupola and decorated with statues and bas-reliefs. The population, almost entirely Dravidian, is very dense as in all the cities of Southern India.

The diocese of Trichinopoly dates back to the time of the early missionaries of the seventeenth century, and until 1923 it covered two regions: the fishery coast evangelized by Saint Francis Xavier and the Madurai mission founded by de Nobili.

As in China, the formation of an autochthonous clergy had been one of the first concerns of the Jesuit missionaries. As early as 1626 Father Vigo submitted a plan for a seminary to the General of the Society for his approval. But his plan was never carried out because of the poverty of the mission and because of endless difficulties, famine, epidemics, and persecutions. By the middle of the nineteenth century, there were still only four Tamil priests.

The first minor seminary was created in 1893 and was annexed to Saint Joseph's College which had been moved from Negapatam to Trichinopoly. It was not until 1921 that the diocese had its own major seminary, which drew its students from the mission, from an apostolic school, and from the college.

The principal obstacle to the development of an auto-chthonous clergy in India has always been the caste system. It is well known that the whole of Indian society was dominated by it. There are the traditional four great castes,[14] which are subdivided into an infinite number of sub-castes. Within these are interwoven different races, heritages, cultures, and professional groups which are foreign and occasionally hostile to each other. The dividing lines are such that Indian Christians have been known to prefer a European to an Indian of another caste or to refuse Communion from a priest for fear of being tainted. In the small town where he was the pastor, Father Monchanin had to struggle against this deep-rooted prejudice. However, since Gandhi's movement in favor of the Untouchables,[15] the barriers between castes have been relaxed and the introduction of western ideas has to some extent favored vocations to the priesthood.

Since 1923, when Pius XI separated Tuticorin from the diocese of Trichinopoly and named the first Indian bishop, Msgr. T. Roche, the diocese of Trichinopoly has been of more reasonable size. It includes 130,000 Catholics out of a population of 1,900,000. Since 1938 it had been administered by Bishop Joseph Mendonça, also an Indian.

This was the religious situation in 1939 when Father Monchanin came to Trichinopoly to begin his Indian life. At first he resided in the bishop's house, where he shared the life of the priests close to the bishop. There, in addition to Father Kalathil, he met Father Arokiam, a young priest who became his teacher and very dear friend. He began at once the study of Tamil. In addition to Sanscrit which is wide-spread but not a living language, Tamil is the only language of India in which complete, traditional instruction in the culture of the country has been regularly given.

> At the Bishop's house I have great freedom of
> mind and the days seem very short. Thanks to the
> zeal of Father Arokiam, I am hoping to do a lot of

Tamil and I am beginning to decipher children's stories. And we talk about everything. He borrowed Masson-Oursel's *L'Inde ancienne* from me, saying, 'I'm going to know India through France'. India is not well known in this house. Hinduism is seen only from the point of view of popular superstitions (which are considerable) without going beyond, behind this thick exterior crust, to the intense numinous feeling concealed in it.

He never completely mastered all the subtleties of the Tamil language, but very soon he was able to read literary works.

I am starting to read more difficult things, *Guru Tales* by Father Beschi. In beautiful Tamil—classical and yet not too mannered (literary texts often contain an excessive use of embellishments). The distance between everyday language and the literary language is enormous. The Christian language is, on the whole, quite successful with de Nobili and Beschi. All, or almost all, of the terms are borrowed from Sanscrit. They are very complete and rich.

Always his prayer and his meditation were centered on India and the Trinity.

I am happy that my first Sunday in Trichinopoly was Trinity Sunday. My life has no other meaning than praising and contemplating this total and unique mystery. India (and unfortunately even Christian India) does not yet know the Trinity, unless perhaps verbally. Who will reveal it? I sense that I am called more than ever. But I do not feel any emotion about it, or even anxiety. My life is a plain without horizon, like the plain here, with a few clumps of trees. I must learn a great deal of patience, in perfect solitude.

The face of India is still hidden from me. I wait, and that is all—and in faith that has been stripped bare. I feel and I know that the more I disappear as an individual the more the Spirit alone will work his way into this India which he wishes to engulf in unfathomable contemplation.

One must be emptied of all that is not the one Fullness. India is learning this. Essentially it has sought only the emptiness and the fullness; and they are the same thing.

30 June 1939, the Feast of Saint Paul

Today is the seventeenth anniversary of my first Mass! In seventeen years I have received many graces from God. It has been given to me to enlighten as well as to orient others in the West, in Judaism, in Islam, and also a little in China. I certainly have to ask God's pardon for so many failings, for wasted time. I would like the rest of my life to be a reparation. God has transplanted me. I am like Jeremiah, when he said, 'I am only a child, I cannot speak.' (Jer 1:6) After having communicated so much—through thought, speech, and writing—I now feel deaf and dumb. I want to sink myself into this silence, to be only adoration and praise. I said good-bye to the West and to everything I so loved there—art and thought—for an unknown land. And I am filled with praise for this land that God has chosen for me. I don't have any idea what I will do. But I have faith in the Spirit. How I wish that from my life and from my death a contemplative life in the Trinity might be born, which will assume, purify, and transfigure all the thought, all the art, and all the millennia of India's experience. I know, I feel, that nothing must be rushed, and I am waiting in patience, for my thought lives almost always in the future.

Those first months spent in Trichinopoly in the solitude created by the barrier of language—the cruel experience of every missionary—was an anticipation of what his life would be like during the next ten years in very remote Indian villages. Father Monchanin was essentially a person who thrived on dialogue and communication with people. It was through human contact and conversation that his thought was stimulated, and no one around him could share in his prayer or fully understand the meaning of his mission. During those often very painful moments, he found great consolation in the depth of his union with God, his love of India, and his intellectual life. He confided to his friend, Edouard Duperray:

> I repeat my thoughts to myself a great deal right now, nourishing myself with my own substance, almost without deep intellectual contact with anyone, and almost without books. I don't want it to be autophagia, but a sinking in of self, with the double meaning of deepening and incarnation.

> It is Hinduism that must be converted, by taking on through mystical substitution (a sea of suffering!) what the spirit of evil and man's refusal have brought about; by reliving in depth and in daily life that *indica praeparatio evangelica*, that Indian preparation for the Gospel, the work of the invisible Word and the hidden Spirit; by placing it, centering, and transubstantiating it in the splendor—beyond all that is given—of the Revelation of the Mystery: the Man-God. Deification of ascending creation, gathered in its entirety into the immutable movement of God, who pours himself out from God and goes to God; articulated Plenitude of the Mystical Body, simultaneously *kevala* and *viśista-advaita* (establishing the immanence of Transcendance as unity is constituted by the Trinity). This has been the vision that renews my strength when I can do nothing more, and the joy

within my sadness.

Another letter written at this time reveals the same desire to penetrate Indian thought so that it will find its florescence in God.

I am doing little else than studying English and Tamil, where my progress is slow. To my delight once again I came across Jean Wahl's *Parmenides* and Eckart's *De Sapientia*, hoping to make a comparison with Indian thought—especially the *Upanishads*. Analogies only. The sources are different and so is the spirit. There is however a similar problematic or rather metaproblematic, a negative ontology that here and there I find more Catharistic than noetic.

I am completely out of touch with Indians (except for children, servants, priests, all of whom are themselves outside Indian thought), and I sometimes feel farther from India than when in Europe. A sort of asphyxia, intellectual asthma. But there is a ray of light. Father Arokiam is becoming more and more attached to me, and he is beginning to become enthusiastic about Hinduism. Through him, I have the feeling that among many Indians, there is a whole world that is concealed and that can be dredged up. Much time and patience are needed, and nothing is foreseeable. When at last I can speak the language, I would like to spend a few days with holy men as a Christian and as one who is initiated into that spirituality which can be disassociated from Hinduism. But would Indians agree to it? And above all what bishop could understand such an experience? But it still seems necessary. Without it I will only know Indian spirituality in a bookish way—intellectual information. I will have the conceptual translation, recognized as essentially deficient, instead of the

> experience itself. It would also be the only chance
> for a deep experience. And it wouldn't simply be
> a pseudo-experience since I would adhere in a real
> way to everything not essentially bound to
> Hinduism—and I think that would be a great deal.
> I love my solitude. I only wish it were deeper,
> above all, fuller.

In September he spent a few days in the mountains at the
Jesuit novitiate at Shenbaganur. There he was welcomed by
Father E. Gathier, one of the great experts in Indian history
and thought. In the years that followed, Father Monchanin
liked to go and rest at that place and in the house where he
found understanding, friendship, conversation with the
priests, and a rich library. There, once again, his desire for
solitude, for silence, and the anchoritic life took hold of him
with particular force. It would be a preparation—if inspired
by the Spirit—for this community of contemplation and study,
this Ashram of the Trinity 'which would gather up all of India
in its oblation in order to trans-situate it: the extasis of the
Trinity prefigured by the unfathomable contemplation of the
Trinity'.

On 3 September war broke out in Europe. The news of it
affected him very deeply. He spent many painful hours, and
for several days he was unable to do any work.

> There is an oppressive silence over Europe and
> over the world. I am following developments on
> the radio and in the English papers. They speak a
> great deal here about the war. It seems very far
> away, as though the distance has been lengthened.
> It is hard for me to turn my thoughts away from
> the suffering of the West. I have the feeling of
> being cut off from the past and from the future, of
> floating in an undefined present. So often we have
> said, 'The war to end all wars.' Today, no one
> even so much as mentions the name of the League
> of Nations in which people had at first put so much

hope. What will humanity be like afterwards? I can't stop wondering about the future, knowing full well that all predictions are useless. Everything must be put into God's hands in unconditioned abandonment: oneself, loved ones, Europe, India, the Church.

Nonetheless I've pulled myself together and am beginning my Tamil again. It is a gentle and subtle language of exquisite politeness and refinement, but its greatest literature will still be inaccessible to me for some time. With Father Arokiam I went to visit some *pariahs* in their thatched earthen huts. They are very poor and humble, very simple, and very happy with the few words we said to them.

A few days later he wrote:

Gloria patri et Filio et Spiritui Sancto!

Invisible future. But I have found peace in this endless blackness. I am offering the world's sorrow. I recapitulate it in the Mass—isn't that *enstasis* in *extasis*? More than ever we have to cling to the Parousia and to live in that final unity. I have the painful impression that in every respect I am standing still, that I am enveloped in a kind of general apathy. The most beautiful desires are in danger of being extinguished in an atmosphere without oxygen—I'm speaking of the external environment. The patience of the earth! I read in Duchesne[17] that Saint Anthony, the first hermit, had his first disciples after twenty years of solitude, he the patriarch of anchorites! India is patient. Let me sink into it, unto death—buried in this reddish earth. But my sadness is not without compensation or hope.

It seems that my ideas are taking flesh within me

and that they are inseparable from the whole of my life which now has *another face.*

In the beginning of November, Bishop Mendonça asked Father Monchanin to accompany him on a trip to visit several Christian centers. It was a way of preparing him for the ministry he was soon to be entrusted with. It made Father Monchanin very happy, and it was a new experience for him, one that took him out of his semi-isolation at Trichinopoly, and which also allowed him to know concretely the way of life of the majority of Indians and to foresee what his own life would be like for many years to come.

He spent four days at Karungulam (black pond), a small village served by an Indian priest who asked Monchanin's help in his parish ministry. From Karungulam, he wrote his mother about the way he spent his days.

> I've been speaking Tamil (badly) with the children and the men. I'm learning more here in three days than in Trichinopoly in a week. The people are very poor and live in tamped earthen huts, thatched with coconut palm. They eat hardly anything except a kind of cornmeal pancake garnished with pimento. Rice is a luxury.
>
> It's very quiet. In the morning I hear the roosters crowing, and in the evening the Indian sisters of the Immaculate Conception chant their prayers.
>
> For the first time I've been hearing confessions! I could understand quite well, especially the children, who enunciate very clearly. I said my three All Souls' Day Masses in this very crowded little church (people come from 8-10 kilometers away) and gave out seven hundred communions and heard confessions for three hours in the morning and two in the evening. Afterwards, a visit to the cemetery accompanied by a tom-tom and a very harsh sounding wind instrument in the

shape of a serpent. In the cemetery (*calarrei*, the room of stone) there was one wooden cross for each dead person. They burn incense at each grave and then cook grain for the poor (probably going back to a Christianized pagan practice: first a meal with the dead and then charity). This cemetery is very moving.

I've been taking short walks with the children who are teaching me the names of trees and medicinal plants.

Returning to Trichinopoly, he found a letter from Father de Lubac awaiting him. It was a great comfort to him to have the following encouraging words about his vocation. 'The memory of you, rather, your presence has been with me constantly. You are nearer to me than when we were both in Lyons, for there is nothing between us now except what is essential. I feel and I live your suffering, your calling, this calling which has thrust you into what might appear to be an adventure, but which is a royal way marked out by Christ—your way. Between us the communion of saints is not without meaning. But it is I who receive everything from it.'

At the end of 1939, Monchanin was still uncertain about his future. From the human point of view, with his immense background, his knowledge of the religious philosophies of India, his rich experience with people and long practice in spiritual direction, he would have seemed destined to a ministry among the elite in the way that had been marked out previously by Ricci and de Nobili. More than anyone, he could undertake fruitful dialogue with Hindu spiritual leaders, as was shown by the contacts he subsequently had with several of them and the deep impression that was made by the papers he read at different religious and philosophical congresses.

Facing this unknown future, he sometimes experienced a feeling of suffocation.

I feel more weighed down than ever, and oppressed, often with the sense that everything is closing in ahead of me. But I also know that it is as it has to be, and that all joy withers.

An unconditioned offering that does not know anything and does not want to know anything. 'Let God be the place for God.' A certain presence intimates that it is his presence.

Totally at God's disposal, Monchanin waited for God's will to be made known to him through the decision of his bishop. In the context of his present situation, he spiritually relived the Mystery of Advent about which he wrote:

Advent calls up the past and anticipates the future, but a past still present and a future already real. Advent is also the heritage possessed in the present.

Entry into the Kingdom of God in spirit. The Mystical Coming of Christ, in the Church and in each of its members, by configuration to his essential mystery and by the presence of the Trinity. An Advent always new, always renewed with each sacramental contact, with each acquiescence to grace, to the call.

Advent gathers up time, projects the past into the future, the future into the past, in the constantly renewed union of a spiritual present where the eternal and the temporal communicate. Man still lives in messianic times and yet already in eschatological times.

The great virtue of Advent: hope.

Shortly before Christmas, Bishop Mendonça informed him of his decision. Father Monchanin was to become curate in the village of Panneipatti. At the end of that year 1939, glancing for a last time over the recent past with its mixture of happiness and sorrow, he expressed what he felt as he entered this new period of his life.

Gratitude for the year that is ending, for the year that gave me India, the land of the Trinity.

FOOTNOTES

1. Emile Sénart, *Essai sur la légende de Bouddha, son caractère et ses origines* 2nd ed., rev. (Paris: E. Leroux, 1882).

2. *L'abbé Jules Monchanin* (Tournai-Paris, 1960) p. 119.

3. *L'abbé*, p. 104.

4. *Dieu Vivant*, (1945).

5. *Entretiens 1955*, Publications de l'Institut français d'indologie, No. 4 (Pondichéry, 1956) 1-10, 23-34.

6. See *L'abbé Jules Monchanin*, and Henri de Lubac, *Images de l'Abbé Jules Monchanin* (Paris, 1967).

7. *L'Eglise naissante et le catholicisme. Le catholicisme des origines à saint Léon*, I (Paris: Le Coffre, 1927) p. 487.

8. The *Petits Frères de Saint-Jean Baptiste* and the *Thérésiennes*.

9. An association of Catholic students interested in helping the missions. It was organized in Louvain by Father Pierre Charles.

10. Pius XI, who died on 10 February 1939.

11. The birthplace of Father Monchanin.

12. *La doctrine morale et métaphysique de Rāmānuja.*

13. The Poor Clare community in Rabat and another community at Bou-Saada in Algeria.

14. Brahman, the priestly; Kshatriya, the warrior or kingly; Vaisya, the mercantile or agricultural; Sudra, the artisan or laboring.

15. In the strict sense the Untouchables do not even fit into the caste system.

16. Jean Filliozat, *L'Inde: nation et traditions* (Paris: Horizons de France, 1961) p. 42.

17. Louis Duchesne, *Early History of the Christian Church, from its Foundation to the End of the Fifth Century* 4 vols., (London: John Murray, 1912) 2:387-390.

FROM VILLAGE TO VILLAGE

Since ancient times, India has had an immense peasant class, and the basic unit, the social cell, continues to be the village. Beyond certain individual peculiarities, village life throughout India is essentially the same.

Villages are made up of small thatched roofed houses built very close together. The narrow streets bordered by covered shops become quite busy toward the end of the day. Animals freely roam the streets having no other place to go. To the north or outside the town there are a few wells set aside for the different castes and a pond for irrigation and ablutions.

The furnishings inside the houses are quite rudimentary: a few kitchen utensils, sometimes one or several rope beds. There are no chairs. People sit on the floor for talking and eating. The food, primarily made from milk, curds, and red pepper is quite unvaried. It is served on banana leaves and eaten with the fingers. Both before and after meals the people purify themselves by means of ablutions. On the whole, Indians lead a frugal life. The peasant population, both men and women, work in the fields from sunrise to sunset. The women must in addition take care of domestic tasks: weave and dye clothes, carry water in huge earthenware or brass jars, cook the food, and take care of the children and the animals.

The very diversified caste system is further complicated by corporate associations which regroup the castes according to professions. This overlapping of social structures is often a source of conflict.

The organization of Christian life in India has had to take these structures and modes of life into consideration. During planting and harvesting time daily life is very curtailed. Mass is celebrated at daybreak, and pastoral visits and other religious services, except on Sundays, take place in the evening when the whole family is together at home.

Shortly before Christmas 1939, Father Monchanin arrived in one of these villages and began to live according to the customs and the standard of living of the people. During the Christmas season he took charge of religious services in a small mission station from Panneipatti called Sinnandipatti, literally 'the village of the small ascetic.' This name was given the place in memory of a Hindu holy man who died there a century ago.

Sinnandipatti, Christmas, 1939

In this little remote village that can be reached only by ox cart, I heard the confessions of the Catholic parish (almost the whole village), and I gave my first sermon in Tamil. Everybody understood—the pronunciation isn't very hard—but I wasn't able to convey any subtleties. I'm not too sure of my vocabulary and I still get tangled up in conjugations. I was very moved by this first Christmas in India. I am going to sink my roots in this land that God has given me.

The pastor of these many villages has asked—with the approval of the bishop—to have me with him. He is a simple man and very apostolic, the only one in the diocese who is working among non-Christians. This is also the only point at which something seems to be taking shape. On the favorable side, I'll be learning non-literary Tamil, and getting acquainted with customs and psychology, and perhaps beginning a communal life (he is in favor of it) that will be recognized by Indians (the seedbed for a group of missionary priests?), and I'll be deeply sharing the life of the Indian people. On the unfavorable side, it will mean a break in my study of literary Tamil which has just got started, a rather rigorous physical life (long trips by ox cart), no possible intellectual contact, the danger of a path that may lead neither to the 'school of Alexandria' nor to a contemplative order. All things considered, I think that I would be refusing the Spirit if I said no. Besides I must show evidence of docility—and that's how it should be. I know through experience that 'God writes straight with crooked lines.' I am filled simultaneously with fear and hope. I must be faithful: to the moment, to the future, to the eternal.

On Christmas Eve, during his midnight Mass, he experienced in an unusually strong way the presence of God in his soul.

Suddenly last night, by the light of the first star, with the crude sound of drums, what a mixture of joy and sorrow, of hope and terror!

Christmas: the Masses, the night, the silence that all the noise seemed to beget within me. How strange it is at each Christmas (and not at any other time) that I am overcome at the Elevation by a burning participation in both the Father begetting the Word and in Mary begetting Jesus Christ. This time it was more intense and more shattering. And the invocation of the *ashram* of the Trinity continues in the chalice of the new and eternal Testament.

A few days later, Father Monchanin was recalled to Trichinopoly to replace a priest who had fallen ill, something

which he often did subsequently. Between 1940 and 1949 he
held about ten different positions as village curate or pastor.
And he was often placed in rather delicate situations where
he had to resolve small schisms brought about by caste
conflicts, smoothe over unpleasantness caused by a predeses-
sor, or reorganize abandoned parishes where no Indian priest
would agree to live. He never refused his bishop.

He spent his free time at Trichinopoly writing down his
first impressions of the popular Hinduism which he encountered in the villages where he stayed. These notes reveal
both the sympathy and the lucidity so characteristic of him
when he spoke of India, its religious thought or its political
problems. Charity was for him inseparable from truth.

Village Hinduism in itself would not be very
enduring were it not for custom (custom is almost
a magical word) and very strong social ties, for it
can be reduced to very little. There are minor
deities about whom no one knows anything—even
their adorers—and they are more or less assimilated, through the theological fiction of 'manifestations', into a great god, *Siva* or *Vishnu*. Everyone
however recognizes *Kadavul*, the sole creator or
rather emitter of the world. The castes are
separated from the *pariahs* (cemeteries and wells).

The unity of India is and must be a creation. It
does not exist as a tangible reality. Even physically
what strikes me is the lack of a plastic quality in
the Indian countryside (plains and mountains). No
architecture stands out (dryness and water—im-
mensity—density). Swarms of people and calm,
consubstantial life and death beget each other. The
myth of *Siva* dancing is the most accurate image of
India. The center is only spiritual. And the unity.
How hard it is for India to incarnate anything at
all. It seems that matter, although so dense, is
not the receptacle for the spirit (nor obstacle, nor
parallel), but rather heaviness thick *māyā*. All this
was alive in me as I was reciting the Christmas

Preface: *ut per visibilia ad invisibilia amorem rapiamur* (that through things seen we may be drawn to the love of things unseen). *'India rapiatur.'* It will take a very burdensome incarnation, and in any case extreme spiritualization, exacting more than elsewhere, asceticism and more than elsewhere contemplation of that which is most essentially spiritual: the Trinity.

On the vigil of the Epiphany, Father Savarimuttu, the pastor of Panneipatti, suggested to Monchanin that they begin a semi-communal life together. Monchanin replied:

I do not have the choice, or the desire to refuse. Nor can I place on it any condition (of duration). I will, very simply, enter into it. And I hope that when the time is ripe, something else will be given to me. May our life together become the seedbed of a more contemplative priestly life, more apostolic, poor, Indian!

Writing to a friend about this suggestion, he explained in detail how he conceived of the communal life.

Here is the plan I suggested to Father Savarimuttu:

Contemplative life: a daily minimum of an hour and a half of contemplation. I don't like precise quantitive limits—each person is unique. However, I believe they are occasionally necessary in community life. Indian priests have been formed in such a regimented fashion that they can't grasp things *in spiritu et veritate*. Office in common, partially. Visit to the Blessed Sacrament (that, too, a recent western form, rooted and felt everywhere as a necessity). Above all, a single orientation: *ad laudem Trinitatis per Christum* (in praise of the Trinity through Christ). Anticipation of the holiness of India (an idea still inaccessbile).

Formation of a special group of the faithful who will devote themselves one day a week to the conversion of India—Saturdays, because of the 'Divine Mother,' who visibly inspires here all *bhakti*.

Intellectual life. Father Savarimuttu is quite intellectual. I would like to suggest our working together a little. He could provide me with the information and I could write a monograph on an Indian village, our own: rural economy (dwellings, agriculture, property laws), sociology (castes and customs), religion (Christian and Hindu, village deities and their relation to high Hinduism). The Brahman from the village who spontaneously offered to give me lessons in Tamil, could be of help. Looking toward future possibilities. The monograph would be under both our names. I think he would like that.

Spirituality. His prayer must be oriented toward the liturgy and toward dogma (the mystics are still inaccessible). I have been praying in English and Tamil with him.

Apostolic life. Be open to experience. Avoid paternalism. If possible raise the level of catechetical work. Require complete sincerity in conversions. Natural contacts. Do not hurry.

Life of poverty. Try for vegetarianism and the standard forms of Indian life. (I'll ask Father Kalathil, the bursar at the seminary, for a list of prices.) In his enthusiasm, Father Savarimuttu has suggested that we give up the parish house in order to turn it into a convent for Indian sisters whom he wants to send for, and we would live under a roof of coconut palms. That would be fine, but I am not sure we would get the bishop's permission. Besides we mustn't seem eccentric.

Indian life. As much as possible.

Even if all that were carried out, it would still be very little and very far from the ideal. But in the beginning we must do just small things—doing before speaking (*coepit facere et docere*). I leave the future to the Spirit coming from the Father and from the Son. I would like so much for this small group of priests to become a kind of third order or *ashram* of the Trinity.

This first plan for a communal Indian life among priests reveals both Father Monchanin's fidelity to what he conceived to be his vocation and his prudence in carrying it out. He was occasionally criticized for excessive or indeed utopian idealism. However high he might have placed his ideal, he never overlooked the concrete conditions for an enduring incarnation of that ideal. His broad experience in spiritual direction had taught him that nothing is gained by forcing nature and that the creation of anything, whether in the spiritual or the temporal order, is the fruit of a slow maturation.

On the feast of the Epiphany he was back in Kulitalai, which was later to become a parish as well as the site of his *ashram*, but in January, 1940 was only a mission station of Panneipatti. In the following months no particular event marked his life. As a curate he spent his time ministering to peasants and craftsmen. His story was, as it would be throughout his life, an inner one, that of the unification of his thought and his spiritual life, of his constant openness to the action of the Spirit. We can follow the unfolding of this life through his meditations on the occasion of several liturgical feasts.

Epiphany, 1940

How I love the Epiphany!

I like the fact that this feast preceded Christmas in

the Eastern Church for more than a century and that it was prescribed in Rome itself.

And these are the Epiphanies of Christ: his birth, his manifestation to the Wise Men, and his baptism. His birth is replaced by the epiphany at Cana (the first sign, that of the metamorphosis of Israel into the Church, according to Origen's symbolism).

The ultimate vision—the *beata temporum plenitudo* (the blessed fullness of time)—from which the duration of the human species and the unfolding of the cosmos are illumined. Does the great theophany (which is told to us from Genesis I to Apocalypse 22: 20-1) not begin with the creation of the cosmic nebula only to be completed in the Parousia? The illumination of this theophany is the baptism of Christ, the first enunciation of the Trinity (that is, according to the Gospels): the voice of the Father and the descent of the Spirit upon Jesus inaugurating His messianic era, manifested as Christ to the Precursor and to the disciples of the Precursor? The Wise Men, the prefiguration of the Gentiles, are the guests at the feast of Israel in Cana of Galilee where the new wine of the Spirit is savored, the very water of the Synagogue metamorphosed. Everything here is the sign of the unique real metamorphosis (from which every being draws its own reality), that of Creation into the person of Christ, the Word uniting into himself man-in-the-universe in order to unite him into the unity of the Three, the unfathomable Circumincession![1]

And it is we who are chosen so that the miracle will continue. Our lives must be the matter of this Epiphany for this part of the world, this geographical triangle, where the glory of the Trinity must shine in its most brilliant splendor, for the illumination of the world! It would take years of silence to lose oneself in this mystery. Glory to the Three and glory to the One.

Conversion of Saint Paul, 25 January 1940

The same introit as for my first Mass: *Scio cui credidi...potens est depositum meum servare* (I know in whom I have believed...He is capable of guarding all that I have committed to him) 2 Tim 1:12. And the Gradual: *Gratia sum quod sum, gratia ejus in me non vacua fuit* (By grace I am what I am, and his grace is not fruitless within me) 1 Cor 15:10. The resounding echoes of these words. What a man saint Paul was, the 'least' of the Apostles, the unconquerable man whom God subdued. It was he who saw the Parousia burning in the depths of his nearly blinded eyes, and the Mediterranean world changed at the sound of his voice.

For a week, I have been living alone—blessedly alone—sometimes taking Communion and Extreme Unction a distance of several miles by ox cart—like men a thousand and more years ago, and over the same land—such small acts of mercy. Most of my time is spent in my room, almost a garret, overlooking a terrace where I can see oxen, cows, goats, women with their brass jars shining on their heads, and at night in complete silence the milky sea of the moon. It seems that little by little India is becoming more at home and quiet within me. The rhythm is the rhythm of things. Man has become reconciled with nature, instead of imposing himself and finally substituting himself for nature. And again it becomes possible to think of God as Creator, *Jam lucis ante terminum, rerum creator poscimus* (Now before the close of day, we pray to you, Creator of all things...)—*Hymn for Compline.*

But if this could only be the starting point toward *Deus absconditus*, the 'hidden God,' who 'siezes' and who is 'seized,' as sudden as a fleeting wind in the deepest crypt of the Caves of Ellora.

8 February 1940

It is Lent, the time of the Church's suffering—with which we must be clothed, in complete ignorance. I am working on a philosophical commentary on the Tamil *Our Father* (a very beautiful one, could it have been written by de Nobili?), trying to find Hebraic, Sanscrit, and also Greek echoes. It opens up immense perspectives. Never have I seen so clearly the grandeur of the *Our Father*. Its form of expression is so Jewish. All those who heard Jesus understood. And no theologian, or mystic, or genius will plumb the depths of it before the glory of the Parousia. That is the prototype of the mission: to propose to all one *mystery* which overshadows the greatest mysteries but in a form so connatural that the most humble person draws his life from it and recognizes in it what is most familiar and most secret in himself.

Holy Thursday, 21 March 1940

In me, too, praise rises up and then falls like a song of sadness. Yesterday I was rereading Foucauld. It was a shock to find him again after more than ten years...a man of uninterrupted prayer who thirsted so for martyrdom (like Andrew or Ignatius or El Hallaj) and who found it in his way. An unfruitful life, a call for disciples (who would be ready to obey anything, to do without everything, to die of hunger), who did not come; plans which were always thwarted; and his fruitful death *nisi granum* [*unless the seed die*]! India demands as much and we must beg for holiness.

Holy Thursday, the origin of the priesthood handed down at the Last Supper: my priesthood, that of my Indian brothers, of my friends. We must now let ourselves be shaped in much patience and through a same Spirit by this Priest, in time and out of time, who divides (*veni separare*) and who unites (*ut dispersos conjugunt*) beyond all else, who died a failure (having served neither Israel nor the world, known only by a few, so little and so poorly known), and who did not see with his human eyes the dawn of Pentecost.

Only one thing is asked of us: an unconditioned gift (may it be once and for all). Our vocation: to prefigure the holiness of India, to think in order to think that, and to be silent in that silence, hard as diamond.

At the time of his first stay in Kulitalai, Father Monchanin had made the acquaintance of an Indian magistrate, *Sri* P. A. Anthony, who had recently been made *tahsildar*, district deputy collector, of this small town of 10,000 inhabitants—of these a thousand were Muslims, a hundred Christians, and all the rest Hindus (a thousand of them Brahmans). Very quickly he became a good friend of this ardent, informed Catholic layman. In the course of a posthumous tribute that appeared in the magazine *Eglise Vivante*,[2] *Sri* Anthony told of meeting Father Monchanin and what the nature of their conversation was.

It was in 1939 that I met Father Monchanin for the first time. He came to my house one evening. I welcomed him as was my custom with a 'Good evening, Father.' He replied, '*namaskaram,*' in the Indian fashion, putting his hands together and smiling. The first thing that struck me about him was his childlike simplicity.

We then began to speak about various matters, touching among other things on the conversion of

India, missionary methods, adaptation, etc. I was thoroughly surprised by his new ideas. He told me he was a great admirer of Indian culture, and of the civilization and philosophical literature of India. He had a special love for the ascetic life of the *sannyāsis* and he himself wished to lead a life of poverty and contemplation. He told of the good work done by two great Jesuits from Bengal, Fathers Johanns and Dandoy, through their journal *Light of the East.* But Father Monchanin preferred to bear witness to the faith by his life and by prayer. Part of his method was to have contact with people of other religions and conversations with them in an atmosphere of sympathy and not of controversy.

Subsequently they often saw each other, particularly to engage in religious discussions. Once when Monchanin spoke of his desire for an eremetic life, *Sri* Anthony offered to help him materially carry it out. Thus the dream that he had had for years was to take shape, and he experienced a very deep sense of joy.

A great source of hope: *Sri* Anthony confided to me that for a long time he had been hoping for a priest who would live 'like a hermit' and exactly as Indians do. If I wish to be this priest, he will build me a small rectory (Indian style), a school, and a dispensary where there will be a Tamil brother. I would live there like an Indian—vegetarian and very simple. It would be above all a contemplative and intellectual life, and I would receive whoever might come, and would talk with Brahmans about spiritual things. It would be called the *ashram*, that is, the monastery. The thought is so beautiful, and so answers my deepest and most constant desires that I cannot believe it. There would be no opposition from the non-Christians (this magistrate says that they would bring me my food themselves), nor would there by any from the

Christians—very simple people, uneducated (most
of them *pariahs*), and very respectful.

The following year (July, 1941), once the bishop accepted
the *tahsildar's* offer, Kulitalai was established as a parish
with the village of Perur as a mission station.   Monchanin
was made pastor and he moved into the rectory that his
friend had built.   He lived there until 1943.

But this still was only an initial step toward the final
hermitage.   Before reaching his Promised Land he would
have to cross years of solitude and a dark night.   It was a
painful exodus; from 1941 to 1945, as a result of the war, he
was cut off from his friends and loved ones in Europe, and
from the communication and conversation with others he so
enjoyed.

During that summer of 1941, when the war spread over all
of Europe, he thought with anguish of the dangers that
threatened the West, the West that had nurtured him intellectually and spiritually and which, in spite of its errors and
failings, represented a store of universal value.   He refused
to believe that it could be engulfed in the waves of some new
barbarism.

I am without news of the war.   All I know is that
Italy has entered this dance of death.   You can
imagine my anguish.   Like you, I am kept from my
work by this almost constant obsession.

But still I do not lose hope for the West.   Force
can know an unexpected triumph, thought can be
suppressed, and the Church driven into the
catacombs.   But force cannot have the last word,
nor thought be extinguished, nor the Church stop
growing, until the Parousia of the Son of Man.   I
believe in the mission of the West, as I do in that
of India, in that of China.   Even torn apart, even
submerged by its perverse elements (all other
elements are guilty to a lesser degree), the West
remains itself with its restlessness which may be

creative (it is in danger of becoming enraged and morbid), its sense of the human, and, in spite of everything, its universalism. But no one knows the time of darkness or the form of the future. The most painful lack is that we have no prophet.

Is not this almost apocalyptic suffering of the present world the most forceful appeal for the coming of the Spirit? And is not the essential requirement to think *sub specie aeterni* (under the aspect of the eternal)? A new unity wants to be born. What is needed for it are souls tough enough to take on the suffering of the world and pure enough to make it transparent in themselves.

More than to any of the other places he lived in India, Father Monchanin was most attached to Kulitalai. He immediately loved this small town nestling in the middle of a grove of coconut palms surrounded by green rice fields. The Kavery River flowed close by. It was quite broad at this spot, swollen by the waters of the great monsoon and blocked off in the distance by a chain of blue mountains. Very often in the evening, when the great heat of the day had lessened and as the sun was setting, coloring everything with soft hues, he would walk along the river meditating and praying. Unlike other poor villages, Kulitalai always seemed to be an oasis favoring recollection and meditation. At times he prolonged his meditations in order to enjoy the quiet calm of the nights and the soft light of the stars. The church and the rectory were located away from the town, and they were surrounded by a small garden which was in bloom all year round, and by thickets filled with birds.

> From my room I hear the bell of a Hindu temple six times a day (offerings of coconuts and rice). Will I be a hermit here someday? Was Foucauld's hermitage cruder still? Life seems too easy here. The water is clear, the rice white, fruit abundant, and one is always delighted to see the trees and to

hear the birds sing. *It is not the place but the soul that counts!* Do I have enough power of concentration? It will take constant prayer and almost uninterrupted meditation. I will have to know Indian thought more deeply—so different from western thought, drawing everything back to an indescribable unity, turned toward the ineffable, a non-knowing, a non-feeling.

It was at Kulitalai that he truly began his pastoral ministry. For many years he was to give himself completely to this ministry among humble people whom he loved and who loved him. His correspondence and his private notes allow us a glimpse of what his life was like, hidden as it was and deprived of human satisfactions.

Fall, 1941

Saturday and Sunday I heard more than a hundred confessions. On Sunday: Mass at eight-thirty and benediction. I have managed, with some difficulty (not having the help of a French-Tamil dictionary and being obliged to make a double translation, through English), to prepare a short sermon. Then two baptisms. The babies were completely naked, wrapped in a fold of their mother's sari. In the afternoon I went to the home of a dead *pariah*, leaving my sandals at the door according to Indian custom. A young man who died of malaria. A very beautiful and calm face that his mother revealed with the light of a small candle. I prayed a few minutes and then had them say the *Our Father* and the *Hail Mary*. They seemed moved by this (unaccustomed) visit. The men were dancing a farewell dance around the body, beating large tom-toms, their faces painted white. Then catechism, managed very simply, and after the evening meal the parish choir with the same percussion instruments.

On Monday, Extreme Unction in a nearby village, trip made in a cart drawn by two zebus (squatting on the floor in the Indian way but with two pillows). This cart like a cradle, thousands of years old. She was a seventy year old woman, quite ready for death.

Today, the second village, farther away, four hours there and back by cart. Going through villages, some Christian, others Hindu, coconut groves, fields of rice or sorghum, small bridgeless rivers, stones, and brambles. But it's not too tiring and there is time to meditate. He was a forty year old man, also ready for death. It is very easy to speak about death here! I was carrying the Blessed Sacrament. I like these long rides in the company of the Eucharist over Indian roads. A village with only two Christian families. Blessing of the house and grain.

What I am doing is infinitely little, the smallest acts of mercy. The rest of the time, I read, I write, I think, and pray and rest too.

October, 1941

I like hearing confessions. You can reach people. My lack of knowledge of the language doesn't allow me to explore very far. And they have very simple minds; the freshness of this simplicity, my only springtime. But they are very sensitive. The Tamils are susceptible, refined, quick to catch a smile, an inflexion in the voice.

Tonight a Hindu festival. The long wailing of a kind of horn which evokes dark mysteries. The goddesses (the people adore goddesses rather than gods) are various forms of the same single divinity manifesting itself under female form, virginal and maternal. God is called mother rather than father.

But she is a fearsome mother, dancing on the bodies of the dead, cruel like their life which couples with death. Her other face is tenderness. Fear and wonder are interwoven, begetting each other like life and death itself. Along with the wailing, the gentle sound of the flute. For them God is not an *idea* but that which they almost touch in an experience obscure to themselves because it is obscure in itself.

I offer myself to God. He alone counts. And he is enough (for the saints). Others desire only that he be enough, and I already feel this desire burning. May India take me and bury me within itself—in God.

December, 1941

I've returned from a tour of the villages. Everywhere a cordial welcome from Christians and Hindus. (Several people told me it was the first time they were able to speak to a priest—those who had come before never had the time or were impatient.) In spite of my bad Tamil, I have been giving sermons all the same. Their lack of knowledge is immense; a surprise, however, to find a Christian happily reading Beschi's Christian poems (very hard) and also Hindu poems. He educated himself all alone in another very remote village. Everywhere there are glimmers. I think they all want to find in a priest, fervor, goodness, patience, and indifference to food and comfort. The faces of Hindus light up as soon as you speak sympathetically about Gandhi.

Except for infrequent visits to Trichinopoly either for his annual retreat or at the request of the bishop, or a few days rest at Shenbaganur, nothing disturbed the quiet routine of his life, which was divided between his priestly duties, prayer, and intellectual reflection. He did not suffer from lack of physical comfort (heat or food) but from the lack of anything from the outside that could have nourished his thinking and sensibility.

> I don't suffer from the heat, and wish it were even greater. Majestic thunderstorms—dry ones. I don't miss bread or wine, but music. It seems as though I have become deaf because I don't hear it. Fill yourself with Bach and Mozart for me, the most precious in Europe along with a few painters, a few poets, a few thinkers, a few saints. India also has music, but I don't have the chance to hear it. The taste of the Catholics has been spoiled by imitating the worst French music, so-called popular songs. If ever I live in a hermitage, I shall try to surround myself with Indian things, to create an Indian atmosphere. But I will have unforgettable memories of Europe.

> I have been reading and writing, and I would like to have a still deeper silence and even painful solitude with God.

At planting and harvesting seasons when the villagers were working in the fields, Monchanin spent his free time improving his knowledge of India and the Indian people.

> India constantly wavers between polytheism (apparently idolatry, the statues of the divinities are bathed each day, washed in milk, decorated, and carried in processions, gods and goddesses are innumerable) and monotheism (all these gods are supposed to be only manifestations of a single divinity identified by some as *Siva* and by others as *Vishnu*) and pantheism (beyond everything a divine impersonality which is the same in God, in man, and in the world and in which everything must ultimately be absorbed). The different systems contain in varying degrees these three elements: polytheism, monotheism, pantheism.

> But they are always more or less recognizable. Indians would not have any difficulty adoring Jesus, but a great deal of difficulty admitting that there is only one God. In the country, much supersition and much fear. Devils play an important role in the popular imagination.

Father Monchanin became daily more attached to the Indian people—through his reading, his human and intellectual contacts, through sharing different ways of life and different economic conditions. 'India is a land that resembles me,' he used to say, 'and I often have the feeling that I was born here and that my ancestors are here. Indians are beginning to think of me as an Indian.' 'In order to know the people well,' he also used to say, 'you have to live a long time in the villages.'

He was very beloved by the people, Christians and Hindus, people of caste or *pariahs* whom he always treated with respect. The kindness and immense patience he showed listening to their complaints and the details of their family quarrels made them feel free to open their hearts to him. Even when he was obliged to speak or to act with firmness (for example, if it was a question of caste prejudice), he could do it with such tact that he was listened to and obeyed. It was for this reason that the bishop sent him into parishes to straighten out difficult situations and restore peace and tranquility. In all the villages he served he made an unforgettable impression. Wherever he went, he was revered as a saint, a *guru*, a *swami* of extraordinary qualities.

Father Monchanin regularly served the religious needs of such small, remote villages as Perur, that could be reached only by ox cart over rocky paths which were sometimes closed off in the monsoon season. The way he spent his time reveals the great hardships he encountered in these mission stations of Kulitalai: Perur, Kallodai, Nellur, Lalapattai, Paneyur. He would arrive toward the middle of the week, visit different families, sharing their simple food, and he would hear confessions for whole days at a time. He admitted that these long periods in the confessional were difficult to endure, with the strong odor of oil that both men and women put on their hair. He would baptize children and care for the sick, often having to make long side trips into the country. At Christmas, for example, he would celebrate midnight Mass, preach, and, still fasting, would set out again for a five hours' ride by ox cart in order to hear more confessions, to celebrate the High Mass, and to preach at Kulitalai. He was not in good health. Severe attacks of asthma made it impossible for him on occasion to celebrate Mass.

Yet he never complained of this exhausting work, of the lack of physical comfort or his poor health. He felt he was still very far from the poverty and renunciation of the Indian people and the *sannyāsis* whose way of life he hoped to share. He also knew through long reflection and personal experience that the cross is the heart of Christianity, the mystery of death and resurrection, that it is the cross that makes man conform to Christ in his redemptive Passion and which is also the condition for the realization of the missionary apostolate. Once when questioned about the problem of evil and the meaning of suffering, he wrote: 'We must embrace suffering and not run away from it.'

Early in the year 1943, Father Monchanin was sent as curate to Panjampatti, a small town located near Kindigul, one hundred kilometers south of Trichinopoly. The pastor was Father Maria-Soosai, a zealous Indian who very quickly became his friend. He remained there until 1945 when he was again named pastor at Kulitalai. He was happy to return to the semi-hermitage which he had liked so much and to his Christian, Hindu, and Muslim friends who had remained very attached to him.

> Every family here, even the poorest (and you can imagine what Indian poverty is like) have been anxious to offer me the first fruits of their rice harvest. I am almost ashamed to accept. But they know that I live like them and through them and

they insist on showing me their gratitude in this
way.

I am feeling very well and have been working (my
ministry is not too heavy, as the parish has few
people in it) intellectually as well. I am colla-
borating with a Tamil priest friend. I love the
Indians and they love me. People of every caste
and religion come to visit me.

I am enjoying solitude and quiet at Kulitalai.
Tropical nights are so beautiful! We are preparing
for the bishop's visit. Masons are white-washing
the poor little church and they are making a lot of
mess. I would like you to see—in your mind's eye
at least—where I am living, the little grove of
coconuts, the houses scattered haphazardly together, and the beautiful tawny human statues.

There was no significant event that troubled his way of
life during the years he spent at Panjampatti and at Kulitalai.
He knew scarcely anything concerning the war other than
what he learned at Shenbaganur where, each year during the
summer, he stayed with the Jesuit Fathers.

In November, 1945 at Panjampatti he met Father Anthony
Fernando, founder of the Rosarian order. It was an
encounter that was to strengthen him in his vocation. The
following are his impressions of his first contact with Father
Fernando.

Father Anthony Fernando is the Indian priest who
founded a monastery of contemplative monks in
Msgr. Roche's diocese (Tuticorin). Their way of
life, which imitates the Trappists, is even more
difficult. Perpetual fast (except Sundays and
feastdays), abstinence (that's not anything—I'm a
vegetarian too, no meat, fish, or eggs, and am
feeling fine), night office, adoration of the Blessed

Sacrament, which is exposed day and night. Manual work, perpetual silence (except for one hour on Sundays). Their great devotion is meditative recitation of the Rosary. Most of them are brothers. He is a priest. He was—even at Panjampatti—an extraordinarily active and zealous pastor and at the age of fifty-five entered the cloistered life. He is very happy and inspires peace. I saw with my own eyes what affection a real priest of God could inspire among Indians. For five days they gave him no rest. He was surrounded by crowds, mothers who brought him their children to bless, old men and women who remembered him. He never showed the slightest sign of impatience, and in spite of all the uproar (Indian crowds are very noisy) he always seemed to be recollected. I admire him a great deal. He preached a triduum, morning and evening. He speaks from the heart, informally and simply, like a father, the same the Curé d'Ars preached. I have never seen so many Confessions and Communions, the return of many sinners. He has come here with me to *Bhakti Ashram* (that is the name of my hermitage, the 'Hermitage of Love'). *He approves of my way of life*, and we are very dear friends.

A few months later, in the spring of 1946, Bishop Mendonça asked Father Monchanin to go with him as secretary and preacher to Rome for his *ad limina* visit and for the canonization of Saint John de Britto, son of an eighteenth-century viceroy in Brazil who was martyred in India by a small local potentate.

The two men left Bombay on 15 August and reached Southampton in the beginning of September. They spent a week in London visiting churches, the National Gallery, and the British Museum where, as they looked at the Indian collections, Father Monchanin explained to the bishop the religious meaning and the beauty of Indian art.

From London they traveled to Lyons, to Lourdes, and finally to Rome where they were received in a private audience by Pius XII. From the Church of Saint-Louis-des-Français, Monchanin wrote his mother about his impressions:

> Lourdes was so much more than I expected. Although there is nothing very beautiful—nothing beautiful at all—the faith of the crowd is moving, particularly that of the sick. And the presence of the Virgin Mary is felt everywhere.
>
> We saw seven bishops. Msgr. Salièges was very nice....
>
> An exhausting trip from there to Rome.... I can't tell you how delightful Rome is. At every corner a bit of the past seems to come alive. Centuries overlap. Palaces and churches (other palaces) are innumerable. Saint Peter's is more beautiful than I had imagined—despite its façade. You should see it for a beatification ceremony. We attended the beatification of Blessed Marie-Thérèse Soubiran, foundress of the Society of Marie-Auxilia-trice. She was a poor saint, misunderstood by everyone, and driven from the convent she had founded.
>
> The Holy Father came to Rome specially for this ceremony. He returned the next day to Castel Gandolfo, and it was there that we met him. He spoke to me in French and blessed my work.

From Rome they returned to Lyons, where Father Monchanin was asked to give a lecture on India at a meeting presided over by Cardinal Gerlier. Present at the meeting were high ranking clergy, university professors, members of the *Société Lyonnaise de Philosophie*, and many believers as well as non-believers. This gathering was a surprise for Msgr. Mendonça. Although he knew that the priest he had taken into his diocese was a very cultivated and holy man, he had been unaware to what extent Father Monchanin was admired and remembered in his home diocese and among this extraordinary audience in front of him. During the lecture there was an electrical failure. In order to divert the audience, which had been led to the heights of Indian thought, Cardinal Gerlier jokingly said: 'Where Father Monchanin is, there is no need for other light.'

Bishop Mendonça set out alone for the United States, allowing Monchanin to extend his stay in Europe. Monchanin decided to return to Paris to see his friends from the Judeo-Christian group, from *Dieu-Vivant*, the *Cercle Saint-Jean-Baptiste*. He had several conversations with indologists and philosophers who were quite amazed by the depth and originality of his insights, although he did not have the training of a specialist.

At Christmas time he visited very dear friends in Algiers and traveled to Rabat upon the invitation of the Poor Clares. These nuns, to whom he had earlier given orientation in the missionary life, subsequently entered the Eastern and Melkite rites in Rabat and Nazareth and became known as the Little Sisters of Galilee.

Monchanin's last weeks in Lyons were spent with his mother, who always remained very close to him. He visited with her in the evenings in her quiet house, and they had long conversations which lasted late into the night.

Toward the end of January, 1947 he embarked once again from Marseilles to return to India, the land of his vocation.

Returning to Trichinopoly, he found that his position had been taken. And through 1947 he was assigned variously as curate and pastor in Trichinopoly (Saint Joseph's) and in several villages of the diocese: Dindigul, Kossavapatti, Mettapatti. At Kossavapatti, he became very ill and was forced to request a replacement.

I did not return to Kulitalai. During my absence a priest who had had difficulties in his parish asked for and obtained that quiet hermitage. I lived first in three parishes in Trichinopoly. Then I was sent to Dindigul to replace temporarily a priest who had become exhausted. It is a busy but interesting ministry. Time is swallowed up. A delightful pastor. Little time free for study.

I'm now at Kossavapatti (Village of Potters), but it is still only temporary. I have the care of 4,000 parishioners, most of whom live nearby, the others to be reached by ox cart. I am acting as pastor until the real pastor's health improves. It will only be after this that I'll have something definite. This village is very quiet and the people—all farmers— are simple. But I have not been here long enough to feel really at home as I did in Kulitalai. The place makes no difference if you are doing the work of the Lord.

We celebrated India's liberation with much joy. The English withdrew with dignity (15 August). Unfortunately since then there has been civil war. In North India (especially Punjab) Muslims and Indians are killing each other. Reading the daily newspaper is heart-rending. Mahatma Gandhi and Nehru are doing what they can to stop the calamity, but they are only partly succeeding. There are two Indias: Pakistan (Muslim) and the Indian Union (Hindu majority). The Christians remain neutral and are not bothered by anyone. Here in Dravidian India it is perfectly calm. The Muslims themselves are quiet. Let's hope that this wisdom will be felt in the North.

In my sermons I have been putting great emphasis on fraternal love, so misunderstood in the present world in India as in Europe.

In June I celebrated my silver jubilee in the priesthood. Twenty-five years a priest! My day

was nothing but thanksgiving. I was at Dindigul.
The pastor invited some of the nearby priests and
they all showed me great affection.

During this period, although he had never sought to make
a display of his erudition, his fame spread beyond the
confines of the diocese of Trichinopoly. He was consequently
invited to Pondicherry—as he often would be later to other
cities—to give a lecture on 'La Crise de l'espérance' to a
gathering of some one hundred Englishmen and Indians.[3]
He later often returned to Pondicherry, either to preach
retreats or to participate in the work of the French Institute of
Indology founded by Jean Filliozat. While there he met
indologists with whom he had intellectual and spiritual conversations, and he spent long hours in the Institute's library
deepening his knowledge of Indian culture. From this period
of collaboration with the Institute, we have two essays, 'Yoga
et Hésychasme' and 'Apophatisme et Apavada.'[4] In his
introductory remarks to the issue, Jean Filliozat commented:
'In these *Entretiens* Monchanin has studied the problem of
hesychasm, *yoga*, and *apavāda*; that is, of apophatic ontology,
which denies to pure being any qualification that would give
it form, aspect, and consequently delimitation and limitation.
For some time the study of hesychasm had caused the
supposition on the part of some authors that the monks of
Mount Athos practiced a type of prayer and contemplation
which might have been influenced by the great technique of
yoga. By carefully analyzing both of them, Monchanin has
brought to light their different nature and allowed us to
understand them better.'[5]

In the beginning of January 1948 Father Monchanin
returned for a third and last time to Kulitalai as pastor. This
made him very happy, preferring as he did his solitude even
to pleasant company. His parishioners, who had been
awaiting his return for some time, celebrated the occasion
with offerings and noisy demonstrations. Then once again

after the festivities, he resumed his quiet life among them.

Three months later Gandhi was assassinated by a fanatic. In him India lost the best of her sons and an irreplaceable leader. This tragic death deeply affected Father Monchanin, who thought with anguish of the future of the Indian people, torn apart by fratricidal struggles and shaken by the effects of modern ideas on traditional beliefs and structures. He joined in the national mourning and publicly gave a eulogy on the *mahatma:*

> In the India of today, so bewildered (Gandhi's death was a terrible loss for everyone; I gave a funeral eulogy in Tamil at Kulitalai and in French at Pondicherry), syncretism is winning out more and more. It seems to me that there are only two alternatives: religious wars, as in the North, or Hindu type syncretism which dissolves all religious and intellectual values, as in the South. Any 'adaptation,' especially intellectual adaptation, is immediately understood as recognition of the equivalence of religions. And any effort to make distinctions, even purely intellectually, is understood as a direct appeal to violence. The political situation is uncertain. And the clergy are, too. On the whole Christianity is pale and without vigor.

For the salvation of India to which he was dedicated, Monchanin buried himself in deeper and deeper silence, prayer and renunciation. He was convinced that only holiness would raise up those apostles that India needed. Holiness alone would reveal India to itself and would quench its thirst for the absolute. He wrote of this to his friend Father Arokiam. The experience of those ten years passed in the midst of the Indian people had strengthened his vocation.

> More and more I think that India will be converted only by holiness. But it will have to be a holiness permeated with sympathetic intelligence (the highest form of charity), and in all its forms it will

have to appear as Indian. There will be much work for future Indians! Let us pray to the Holy Spirit whom India is awaiting, that Spirit who melts all that is rigid and who penetrates beyond the thickness of the letter to the depths of God.

Consistent with the Incarnation, which is not merely adaptation but assimilation of existence, sensibility, thought, and which is communion in hope and the deep spiritual concern of those who are to be saved, he had decided to share totally the condition of this people who were the 'portion of his inheritance'. From the human point of view, the fruitfulness of this hidden life might seem slight. This is particularly true when we think of the exceptional gifts which were his. For his friend Joseph Folliet, he was 'one of the greatest, perhaps the greatest member of the French clergy between the First World War and today.'[6] But Monchanin had learned through long personal experiences that all spiritual fruitfulness requires a kenosis.[7] He also knew that it is in the night of the earth, where it must first die, that the seed will be reborn and bear fruit. This was the conviction which had caused him previously to give up a brilliant university career in order to live among workers in the outskirts of Lyons. And it was that same certainty that all redemption goes through solitude, renunciation, and suffering which had led him to embrace the life of those who were 'despised and rejected', for whom he always had a particular love.

These ten years had also allowed him to compare his ideas about India with the hard reality of India which he discovered in his daily life and in contact with the very poor—Christians and Hindus. It was a long and bitter purification, but one that prepared him even more than his studies for 'that which was now to be given to him'.

FOOTNOTES

1. Circumincession: the tension of communion within the Trinity.

2. January-February 1958, pp. 52-3.

3. See *Eglise Vivante*, I, 1 (1949) 18-35; *France-Asie*, 79 (December, 1952).

4. *Entretiens, 1955*, Publications de l'Institut français d'indologie, No. 4 (Pondichéry, 1956) 1-10, 23-34.

5. See *L'abbé Jules Monchanin*, pp. 104-108.

6. *L'abbé Jules Monchanin*, p. 54.

7. The term of Saint Paul, the emptying of self, Ph 2:7.

THE ASHRAM AT KULITALAI

FATHER MONCHANIN BEGAN in 1947 to correspond with Henri Le Saux, a Benedictine monk from Saint Anne de Kergonan Abbey in Brittany. Le Saux had been hoping to go to India to introduce a monastic life which would be both Indian and Benedictine. Once Bishop Mendonça had agreed to accept him in his diocese and had approved his plan, Father Monchanin wrote to him:

Trichinopoly, 7 August 1947

Filled with the joy of the Holy Spirit I am writing you in the name of Bishop Mendonça, who has just returned from Europe and America. Your letter reached me like a reply from God. Since May 1939, I have been in the diocese of Trichinopoly. Bishop Mendonça in his great kindness has been like a father to me. I have learned English and Tamil. My ministry is now in a small parish, where I am much more hermit than pastor.

If you come here, the bishop would like us to begin together a life of prayer, poverty and intellectual work. Study English as much as you can. You won't object to the purely vegetarian diet (necessary for the life of a *sannyāsi*). It will take steadfast courage, because you will have disappointments, total renunciation of western things, a deep love of India. The Paraclete will give you these three gifts. I am waiting for you. India is waiting for you. A Tamil priest friend will join us soon, I hope. Prepare yourself in prayer and oblation of self. In Him you are my very dear brother.

A few months later he wrote:

Dear Father and brother in Our Lord,
I hope it is not too late—almost the last day of the month—to wish you a happy New Year. There hasn't been any news from you for some time. I have been quite ill—a severe asthma attack. I am almost back to normal. Once again, through the kindness of our bishop, I have returned here to Kulitalai. I am waiting for you here, for you have decided, I hope, to answer the call you have heard for fifteen years to become an Indian in India. We can begin together. I will initiate you into life in India and you will initiate me into Benedictine life, for I strongly agree with you that the patriarch of the West must also in the plan of God become the patriarch of the East. His rule, taken at its source, is flexible enough to be adapted to all situations and all spiritualities. In this regard, I want to draw you attention to a beautiful passage by the late Father Mersch in *La Théologie du Corps Mystique*, II, pp. 234-235. Doesn't that define our whole way of Life?

He added a few practical details about schedules and traveling expenses, what administrative steps to take, what books and clothes to bring, and he concluded his letter with the following words:

We will have to begin very simply. It will only be
later that we can make rules. There will be native
vocations, but few at first. *Alius est qui seminat
et alius est qui metet* (There is one who sows and
another who reaps); we will have to begin with
great hope.

Father Le Saux disembarked at Colombo on 15 August
1948, a symbolic date, the feast of the Assumption and the
anniversary of India's liberation.   After a short stay in
Trichinopoly, he traveled to Kulitalai and lived in the rectory.
There Le Saux and Monchanin prepared for their future foundation by a communal life, prayer, study and exchanging
ideas. In the beginning of 1950 they left the rectory to live in
flimsy cells made of bamboo and thatch in a mango grove
along the bank of the Kavery River. They neither owned nor
rented, but were merely authorized to live there temporarily.
Later, they were obliged to move, finding the place unfit for
health, infested with snakes, scorpions, and monkeys whose
noisy cries during the night disturbed their sleep and their
recollection.
   On 21 March 1950, the feast of Saint Benedict, the
patriarch of western monasticism who must also become the
patriarch of eastern monasticism, the official foundation of
the *ashram* was marked by a solemn Mass.   And on 11
October of the same year, the feast of the Motherhood of
Mary, the small rustic chapel was blessed. It was a small
brick room with an altar and a tabernacle of solid un-polished
granite, recalling the architecture of Hindu temples. It contained no decoration: image of the emptying of the soul
before the Absolute. The chapel was located at the entrance
to the hermitage, making it possible for the Christians from a
small nearby village to attend Mass and to adore the Blessed
Sacrament.
   Relieved of the parish at Kulitalai, Monchanin was from

that time on able to lead fully the life of a hermit. But his contemplative vocation, as we shall see, was not to separate him from men.

This humble monastic foundation, focusing on a Trinitarian spirituality and prefiguring the holiness of India, began as a response to his personal calling, which we have seen emerge in the preceding pages. Shortly before his first departure for India, Monchanin had written to a nun who had been brought up at the Balmont Orphanage where he had been chaplain and whom he had directed toward the religious life:

> Pray to the Holy Spirit that I will one day be a monk in a monastery born from the thought, heart, and contemplation of India and dedicated to the Holy Trinity. That is my constant thought and my one essential wish.

> I am delighted that you are a nun and that you are dedicated to the Only One who is worthy of being sought. Live the words of Saint Bernard: 'The measure of loving God is to love him without measure.'

> Bury yourself in silence and contemplation (but all the while remaining thoroughly young and spontaneous). God loves the free heart of a child. Your memory is with me as I go and I shall pray for you in India, that you become a *saint*, the only thing that counts. You must not want anything less than that. That is the only peace and the only joy.

Contemplation incarnated in Indian forms seemed to him to be an absolute necessity for the conversion of India. This was the conclusion after long reflection and his missionary experience:

> Everything I see around me, whether among Christians or Hindus, convinces me more and more

about the necessity of a contemplative life in India. Although there are some ten Carmelite Monasteries for women, there are at present only about twenty or thirty Carmelite monks in India, and all of them on the west coast (Malabar). Most of them are not strictly contemplatives and they are all too Europeanized in their mode of life and way of thinking. There certainly is a place for other religious who are Indian in spirit and customs, who will adore God in the name of the whole of India and who will endeavor to rethink India as Christian and Christianity as Indian. That is our wish, that our vocation. Before God I have meditated on it a great deal invoking the Holy Spirit, and I deeply believe that it was for that I was born.

Our goal: to form the first nucleus of a monastery (or rather a *laura*, a grouping of neighboring anchorites like the ancient laura of Saint Sabas in Palestine) which buttresses the Rule of Saint Benedict—a primitive, sober, and discrete rule. Only one purpose: to seek God. And the monastery will be Indian style. We would like to crystallize and transubstantiate the search of the Hindu *sannyāsi*. *Advaita* and praise of the Trinity are our only aim.

This means that we must grasp the authentic Hindu search for God in order to Christianize it, starting with ourselves first of all, from within.

Ultimately, for Monchanin the growth of the Church demanded that it be present—and in India more than elsewhere—in its highest form: institutionalized contemplative life. Pure adoration is its essential function. It was for this reason that 'as a spiritual society, it was essentially set apart...an adoration which is but anticipation, a foretaste and "rehearsal" of eternal life in the heart of the Trinity'.[1]

In the first chapter of the *Ermites du Saccidānanda*,[2]

Monchanin speaks eloquently of the place and role of the contemplative in the Church. Without the contemplative, the Church would:

> lose its radiance, be weighed down in the con-
> tingent realities of earth—a weight then too heavy
> ever to be lifted by the leaven of eternity. Without
> the contemplative, the eyes of the Church would
> be veiled to the horizon of the ultimate future,
> which alone, finalizing the meaning of the world
> and of history, confers on it its total meaning....[3]

But this new type of foundation inevitably evoked surprise and opposition among those around them, primarily in the ecclesiastical world. History teaches that in both the human and spiritual orders geniuses, reformers, and saints have been signs of contradiction. Father Monchanin knew this to be a fact, having experienced it in the course of his ministry in France. He spoke freely of it in a letter written to Father Duperray on Pentecost, 1951:

> Our very insignificant *ashram*—just the two of us,
> a wandering *sannyāsi*, a brahman philosopher who
> occasionally shares our life, and an eccentric and
> yet very perceptive old Christian pensioner whom
> we will not keep and who is already quite a local
> legend—is considered suspect by the Jesuits, who
> strongly influence opinion (some are my very
> faithful friends). Will the forthcoming publication
> of our pamphlet on the meaning and goal of the
> *ashram* alleviate or aggravate their fears? At least
> no doctrinal investigation has yet begun (and we
> would appear to be still more suspect in that than
> in our way of eating and dressing). All this is
> normal, to be expected. Indian Catholics have
> been told that Hinduism is a diabolic invention too
> long for them not to be surprised or disconcerted
> by an understanding and sympathetic attitude.
> And the theological and philosophical level of the

secular clergy (and even the regular clergy) is too
elementary for our intellectual and spiritual
positions to be welcomed or even understood. We
must, in silence and patience, be hidden and
unheard witnesses of something whose vastness
and exact outlines, and most secret meaning we
ourselves do not know and will perhaps never
know.

It was thus in order to avoid any confusion concerning
their work and its goal that Fathers Monchanin and Le Saux
published, a few months later, a slim volume 100 pages long,
entitled *A Benedictine Ashram*.   In it they justified
theologically their position both in the Church and in India. It
is necessary to quote large sections from the first chapter, for
the problem involved is considerably more than merely an
Indian one.   It also exists in other missionary situations,
particularly at this time when there is a danger that under the
impact of technical civilization and the desire for immediate
and visible results, the hierarchy of values may be forgotten.

The spiritual society that is essentially set apart for
such an end (the glory of God) is the Holy Church,
the Spouse and the real Mystical Body of the risen
Christ. The Church is above all dedicated to God
and stands as his witness to the same degree as it
is consecrated to pure adoration. Thus the first
goal—and duty—of the Church is adoration. Contemplatives within the Church contemplate in its
name, taking their prayers from its divinely
inspired liturgy, sharing through their thoughts in
its faith, and through their love in its burning and
consuming charity. For them, the very apostolate
itself is entirely dependent on contemplation as its
source, or is even identified with it (as in the case
of purely contemplative orders). [4]

Of the Church in mission countries, it may well be
said that the birth of contemplative orders is one

of the sure signs of prolific growth. Contemporary missiology has emphasized that the aim of any missionary activity is to implant the Church in a particular territory. As long as the new plant has not taken deep root, indigenous orders will not sprout freely. But once the plant has grown, then the sons of the soil are made its spiritual leaders. Indigenous priests and bishops govern the local churches, organic units within the ecumenical Church.

Indeed, each local church—in so far as it constitutes a relative 'autarky' (independent unit) —ought to be a faithful image, a true miniature of the universal Church. [5]

Thus it must be fully endowed, not only to save men but also and above all to praise God, as an individual member of the Mystical Body. A local church deprived of the necessary means to fulfill its primary task, that is, contemplation, without its own contemplative orders, would appear—and in fact would be—an incomplete and mutilated Church. [6]

Christ expects of each land and of each people an outburst of praise and love, which they alone can offer him. Very often the Church is compared by the Fathers to the *polymita tunica* (the coat of many colors—Gen 37:3) of the patriarch Joseph, to the splendidly adorned mantle of the bride of Solomon *circumdata varietate* (Ps 44 [45]:15). A particular type of Christian spirituality has to evolve out of the particular genius of the people of each country. The qualitative universality of the Church, nowhere foreign, never outdated, but contemporary with every age and connatural with every civilization, is but the final harmonizing and synthesizing of all civilizations, assumed by Christ, the absolute Man, into his theandric pleroma. [7]

India cannot be alien to this process of assimilation by Christianity and transformation in him. It has stood for three millenia, if not longer, as the seat of one of the principal civilizations of mankind, equal to if not greater than that of Europe and China....[8]

For centuries India was the most advanced civilization, spiritually and intellectually dominating the surrounding countries and even the Far East: Ceylon, Burma, Tibet, Central Asia, Indonesia, Siam, Indochina, and Japan. Today, reawakened and independent, it wishes once again, for the peace and good of nations, to assume its ancestral leadership. We can say that India is to Asia what Greece was to Europe, and the message it has to give the world is similar to the message of ancient Greece. That is why, in its aims and in its methods, the Christianization of Indian civilization is a historical undertaking comparable to the Christianization of Greece.

Besides, India has received from the Almighty an uncommon gift, an unquenchable thirst for whatever is spiritual.[9] Since the time of the *Vedas* and the *Upanishads*, countless numbers of its sons have been great seekers of God.

Century after century there rose up seers and poets singing the joys and sorrows of a soul in quest of the One, and philosophers reminding every man of the supremacy of contemplation: 'upward' and 'inward' movements (*extasis* and *enstasis*) through knowledge (*jñāna*) to the Ultimate (*para-nirguna-Brahman*....[10])

We may think quite rightly that such a marvelous seed was not planted in vain by God into the heart of India. What Saint Justin Martyr and the philosopher Clement of Alexandria said about

Greece may well be applied to India. The Logos
mysteriously prepared the way for his advent, and
the Holy Spirit from within stimulated the search
among the purest of the Greek sages. The Logos
and the Holy Spirit are still at work, and in a
similar way, within the depths of the soul of
India.[11]

Unfortunately Indian wisdom is tainted with
erroneous tendencies and does not seem to have
found its own equilibrium. So was Greek wisdom
before Greece humbly received the paschal
message of the risen Christ. Outside the unique
revelation and the unique Church man is always
and everywhere incapable of sifting truth from
falsehood and good from evil.

But once Christianized, Greece rejected its ancestral errors—mostly its too cosmic outlook and the
neglect of the Absolute in its transcendental
aspect—and, baptized in the blood of its martyrs,
it became the leader of the world in philosophy,
theology, and mysticism. So also, confident in the
indefectible guidance of the Church, we hope that
India, once baptized into the fullness of its body
and soul and into the depth of its age-long quest
for *Brahmā*, will reject its pantheistic tendencies
and, discovering in the splendors of the Holy Spirit
the true mysticism and finding at last the vainly
longed-for philosophical and theological equilibrium between antagonistic trends of thought, will
bring forth for the good of humanity and the
Church and ultimately for the glory of God
unparalleled galaxies of saints and doctors.[12]

Should India fail in that task, we cannot understand humanly speaking, how the Mystical Body of
Christ could reach its qualitative and quantitative
fullness in his eschatological coming.[13]

India has to receive humbly from the Church the sound and basic principles of true contemplation, to keep them faithfully, to stamp them with its own seal and to develop through them along with the other members of the Church. Authentic Christian contemplation is built on the unshakable foundation of revealed truths concerning God and man, and their relationship together.[14]

When *A Benedictine Ashram* was published, Father Monchanin sent a copy to Edouard Duperray and, emphasizing the spirit in which it had been written he wrote to his friend: 'I want this book to be irenic: the call for an *ashram* where Indian thought and Christian thought will be studied with respect and love, with the awareness of the mystery which overshadows us all.'

The work was, however, welcomed sympathetically by missionaries and Indian priests.

Our pamphlet is gaining ground in India. I have already received many encouraging replies; a few even were moving (Father Dandoy, Arango, Animananda, Meyersen, etc.), some emphasizing poverty and others adaptation. The Carmelites and the Rosarians replied warmly.

The bishop also had given his blessing to their foundation and considerable encouragement to the two priests. Many times in the years to come he was to defend them in face of criticism from less understanding bishops.

Msgr. Mendonça is extremely kind to us, heartily approving our 'innovations' a few of which are rather daring. We are fortunate to have him as our bishop. Other bishops might not show us as much confidence. We wrote a long statement for him which spells out in detail our goals and spirit. He had it examined by two Jesuit theologians and approved it all. So now we are definitely 'committed' to this new way—I have been yearning for it for ten years—but we are the first to see the possible dangers in it: deviation or incomprehension.

It was with utmost discretion that Monchanin and Le Saux undertook their hermetic life, anxious as they were not to lay themselves open to further criticism. Once they were settled in their new property at Kulitalai, they also had to take care not to interfere in parish matters with which they were no longer directly concerned. Father Monchanin had learned through his long stay in villages, where Christians were at times divided among themselves, that it was necessary to stay out of their domestic quarrels and to intervene only if they gave cause for scandal or un-Christian witness to the Hindus. As early as 1950, he had brought this to Father Le Saux's attention:

> We must have our full independence and we must be on good terms with our neighbors. We can expect criticism. Our way of life and thought calls for it.
>
> Besides, it seems to me that we must adhere to three inflexible rules:
> 1) Never intervene directly or indirectly in parish life, whether it concerns persons or things.
> 2) Absolutely refuse to take up or even listen to the grievances of parishioners. In order to do this, from now on observe *silence* in the *ashram*. At most only engage in those conversations which are exclusively spiritual (confession and spiritual direction).
> 3) Never reply to indirect criticism.
> These are the absolutely necessary conditions for our peace and perhaps even for our existence as ashramites.

Despite their prudence they were in fact criticized, as was mentioned above, for their austere life, their friendly relations

with Hindus, and their innovations. De Nobili himself had
not gone quite so far in intellectual adaptation. Gradually
prejudices lessened, particularly among visitors to the
ashram, who were struck by the charity and humility of the
two men. The support they received from Msgr. Mendonça
also played a large role. In 1951, Monchanin wrote to
Edouard Duperray:

> We are now warmly welcomed and among certain
> individuals even enthusiastically. Similar hopes
> are being nurtured by many. Some Jesuits who
> had been cool toward us for over a year have
> become once again courteous and even cordial.
> The Archbishops' Conference has officially ap-
> proved our wearing the *kavi* 'as an experiment'
> and 'for a chosen few, mostly for the contem-
> plative ones.'

The *ashram* was well thought of by Hindus in the area.
Soon spiritual persons of many beliefs came for visits and
spent time there, drawn by the quiet of the place, the
brotherly welcome of the two priests, and their love of silence
and contemplation. Father Monchanin frequently alluded to
this in his correspondence:

> A Hindu, who is a *Brahman-sannyāsi*, has been
> with us for two weeks. He is a pure *advaitin* who
> continually reads and meditates on the *Upanishads*
> and judges everything in light of them. I have no
> idea what our living in common will produce if it
> continues. But it is already remarkable that such a
> person accepts our life....
>
> A few Christians and a few Hindus (Brahmanic)
> visit us. I speak about God to all of them....
>
> Two *sādhus* came recently. One of them, a

Buddhist from Ceylon who was converted to mystical Hinduism has combined *Vedānta* with *Śaivasiddhānta*. (That is very common here where 'all religions are lost in the Absolute like rivers in the sea'.) He has travelled throughout all of India from *ashram* to *ashram* and he told me that nowhere else did he find as much *shanti* (peace) as here, the sign of divinity. Trees make a great deal of difference too. It is true that in many *ashrams* visitors are often somewhat rude and talkative. We hope to bring to India that true inner peace which it so loves! He also told me that he has never met a mystic—although he has sought at great length—who has reached the fourth state (the transcendent state, the constant and conscious realization of ultimate identity). This would be in some way the Hindu equivalent of the spiritual marriage—the state of theopathy—of Christian mysticism. Something very rare. It is also Spinoza's 'knowledge of the third type'—*sub specie aeternitatis*—which, according to Lachièze-Rey, 'is the knowledge of no man'. He is a saint of this type, theopathetic and yet able to translate at the level of thought—*aliquo modo*, by inverted analogies—his pure intuition of God.

I was also visited by an extraordinary *sannyāsi*. He told me that he had never met anyone, *guru, sannyāsi* who was *the one he was seeking*. He told me of his deepest personal difficulties, his spiritual isolation. He seemed very sad, although peaceful. When he left he asked me to bless him, and there were tears in his eyes....

Without his seeking it, he aroused in others a deep and spontaneous confidence. When he was still in France, several people wrote him that they had felt the presence of God through him. This spiritual presence which radiated from him was merely the outpouring of his own interior life.

Christians, Hindus, non-believers who visited the *ashram* had at times the same impression after having talked with him. They discerned through his words, his attitude, and his prayer, a Presence which enveloped him and radiated out on anyone who was with him.

Such contacts and conversations with different *sannyāsis* gradually revealed to him the greater and greater riches of the Indian spirit. He admired even among the peasants whose faith was blunted by rather crude superstitions, the courage with which they endured their miserable life and their detachment from temporal things. He wrote in 1951 the year when India underwent a nearly total famine:

> The people suffer and wait. There is an almost
> unlimited capacity for resignation and patience in
> the Indian soul. Time counts so little. It is much
> easier than in the West to see things and history
> from the point of view of eternity.

He concluded—and this conviction would be a strength for him during his first efforts and the long wait for disciples—that India more than any other continent was marvelously prepared spiritually to receive the Christian message—if it were presented in Indian forms, stripped of everything accidental which centuries of history had added. Yet we shall see later that after having compared his theoretical ideas with the hard reality of daily life and after having more deeply studied the various systems of Hinduism, he will acknowledge the human impossibility, if not of converting individuals, at least of seeing the formation of a specifically Indian Christian thought. 'He no longer saw how it could remain typically Indian.'[15]

In the beginning of 1952 Father Monchanin was asked by the Canadian Holy Cross Fathers to Barisal, East Pakistan, to preach a retreat. In the years to come he was often invited to undertake this type of ministry. These invitations clearly show how highly superiors of religious orders thought of him and how much they appreciated his teaching and spiritual counsel. Even though some ecclesiastics criticized his experiment in Indian monasticism and remained sceptical about the future of the *ashram*, no one doubted the depth of his religious life. Visitors at Kulitalai were won over by his perfect politeness and profoundly impressed by his asceticism and his charity. Once they saw him and his way of life, they were quick to change the preconceptions with which they had come.

The central theme of his retreats to contemplatives was the mystery of the Trinity. His talks occasionally went on so long that he lost all sense of time, even meal time.

This ten-week trip to Pakistan and the North allowed him to discover India in its linguistic, ethnic, and spiritual diversity, but also in its unity.

In his travel diary, he wrote of many things: the emotions he felt visiting various shrines, the internal situation of the regions he crossed, as well as the currents of thought influencing young university students:

> *East Pakistan* [*Barisal*], with the French Canadian Fathers. They are doing very fine social and (indirect) apostolic work. Great sense of teamwork and youth. This has caused the opposition of the older men (the inert ones and the partisans of an apostolate *opportune et importune* ('in season and out of season': 2 Tim 4:2). It is a continuing crisis.

> What is so tangible here is the error of the theory of 'two nations' which gave rise to Pakistan, the 'land of the pure'. It is the same people on one side of the border as on the other. The desire to Islamize makes the eastern half of this people inflexible. Much blood has flowed. Fear still remains. My heart breaks seeing so many Hindu houses deserted and the land deprived of leadership due to this exodus.

> *Calcutta*. An Indian city of 6 or 7 millon people

including outskirts and refugees. Misery and
luxury go hand in hand. The Bengali elite are cultivated, passionate, even quarrelsome, and un-
stable. All types of art and thought are mingled.
The young people don't seem at all sure what to
take up. Many (the most generous) of them turn
to Stalinist or Trotzkyite Communism. Hinduism
is weakening and disappearing—*Brahmo-Śamāj*
and the Ramakrishna Mission.[16] Art reflects—
without much brilliance—all the tendencies of the
East and of the West (even surrealism). Practical
materialism (trade, money, the desire for the easy
life) is very widespread. Yet in all this, certain
persons have found true Christianity. I met two
students who came to Christ, one through the poet
T. S. Eliot and the other through the philosophy of
science. The first was for a long time a Marxist
theoretician who absorbed everything: Marx,
Lenin, Stalin! The son of Ananda Coomaraswamy
was also converted.[17] He comes each morning
with his wife to the small chapel of Father Fallon
and Antoine, the two intellectual apostles of
Bengal. Father Dandoy is still working.

The holy places of Buddhism (also of Jainism):
Rājghir the famous, ancient city of Rājagriha
where the first council of Buddhism was held. It
fell into great decline and is now a poor and ugly
village with a few ruins and more recent Jain
temples.

Nālanda, now the site of excavations of the
famous university where Hiuang-Tsang[18] was
initiated to the *Mahāyāna*. A huge and very
beautiful *stūpa* (sculptures from the 8th and 9th
centuries). A Hindu converted to Buddhism (not
unusual) is going to build a *Pāli* institute in
Nālanda itself. It is impossible to describe the
grandeur of these ruins which cover several miles.

Bodh Gayā where Buddha received the *bodhi* under the *pipāla*. A *pipal* is still there! A great holy place visited by Burmese, Cingalese, and Tibetans. I meditated too under this *pipal*!

Sarnath with the beautiful *stūpa* of Asoka[19], a stele still very legible and a small museum (a masterpiece of good taste), which houses extremely beautiful Buddhist sculpture. On the different pieces you can follow the progressive absorption of Buddhism by Hinduism.

Benares. A whole week. And it is still not enough for visiting this unique city, where each sect, each *ashram* has its center: Hindus of all types, Buddhists, Jains, Sikhs, Muslims, Christians. It lacks only a synagogue and a Parsi temple.

The Temples of Khajurāho. Some of the most impressive and in a desert setting. Powerful, ordered architecture. I was housed in a Jain temple (at Rājghir in a Buddhist temple).

Agra, a wonder of Islam. Strength and grace, light and shadows. Purity of number and perspectives (Taj-Mahal and tombs).

These brief travel notes—and there are many more—reveal Monchanin's lucid and sympathetic curiosity about the traditions and expressions of Indian culture. His contemplative vocation, as we have said earlier, was incarnate contemplation, rooted in what is most essential and most permanent in India. The missionary vocation was, according to him, a unifying option, which implies, like any choice, exclusion and subordination: exclusion of everything (even excellent) which would be incompatible with this calling and would burden it; subordination of the whole and of the details of activity, all thought, feelings, and spiritual life itself, to this desired and hoped-for end. Thus throughout, and to the very end of his life, he dedicated himself to India.

But even though his contemplative vocation was 'neither an escape nor a Garden of Eden'; his gift to India did not turn him away from other spiritual continents, their problems and their suffering.

China, Islam, and Africa remained close to him through the missionary vocations which he had helped to orient. And through prayer and the offering of his own sufferings, he was in communion with the Church's passion in these lands. We find the echo of this spiritual concern in his correspondence with a nun, originally from Lyons, who had spent twenty years in the religious congregation founded by Father Lebbe. She was the first European nun to have been juridically placed under the authority of an autochthonous religious superior. Recalling the unfortunate death of a member of the International Women's Auxiliary in Nanking, Monchanin wrote to her:

> Her death as a witness to Christ and to his universal love counts more than anything else for the renewal of the Church. And Father Bede Tsang, whom we used to know and who did a remarkable thesis in Paris on the origin of Chinese characters (using the views of Fr Jousse), also died in the silence of his prison. Witnesses that the Church raises up in the twentieth century Church.... The Chinese Church is the 'salt of the earth'.

> I am united with you in your prayer from Rabat. On the horizon of Islam another people, unknown to itself, awaits the mediator, a people as inaccessible to Christian apostles as the Soviet world and even more so! As you say, we need saints.

A few months later he continued to encourage this nun, who had been driven out of China and cut off from her congregation, to remain faithful to her original vocation:

> I think you are quite right to turn down the requests from Hong-Kong and instead to go quickly to Formosa. It will of course be up to you 'to plant out the rice in Father Lebbe's rice field'. What is more important, more important than any hospital work, is to preserve at any cost the spirit of his foundation, the dedication to poverty, the way of praise and contemplation, brotherly love. With Sister Chao and your two Chinese sisters, you will be the seed that will bear great fruit in Chinese soil....
>
> I am delighted, dear Sister, that you have more time for the contemplative life than previously. In a so-called inconvertible environment we are not without power. Fulfilling in ourselves our brothers' search for God, we unify it in Christ and present it as sacrifice to the Father in the Spirit. You too must offer the implicit prayer of this Formosan people whom you have adopted. Wait in luminous peace, anticipating in yourself their salvation and their return to the Holy Trinity. Soon of course, God will give you novices filled with this spirit of an apostolate through contemplation.
>
> I think of you wherever I am. You are far away and yet very present to me, whether at Pondicherry, or at Madras, where the light was so beautiful.

For Fathers Monchanin and Le Saux, the year 1953 began with great hope. Two months later a Belgian Cisterican, who had been thinking of going to India since 1938, informed them of his desire to join them and to share their monastic and apostolic life. Monchanin wrote of this happy news to Father Le Saux, who was at that time absent from the *ashram:*

It is very true, as you say, that if he came and especially if Father Dharma came too, it would be a real beginning. Solitude weakens or degenerates without a bare minimum of communal life. And Indians who don't believe in our way of life and who find us fanciful would be more attracted by a monastery which was even provisionally constituted. The nucleus of Europeans still seems to be the indispensable means of transition.

As we wait for God's good time—or for some completely different and unforeseeable way—may the peace of the Spirit remain with you. The rhythm of India is slow—pay no attention to ironical smiles and their questions, 'How many of you are there?' Only one thing counts: continuing to be free and open.

A few days later, a German Benedictine requested information about the *ashram*. Other monks in the course of the following years were to be attracted by this type of incarnate contemplation. But the very positivistic central government of India refused to grant visas, scarcely treating *sādhus* any better than missionaries, especially Christian *sādhus* which it considered social parasites.

The same hope and the same uneasiness appeared again in a letter to a friend written the following year:

Our *ashram* is always keeping vigil, an Advent. A Bengali convert is to join us. He is an ex vedantist, ex-Marxist who wanted to write a book that would make Marxism irrefutable. He became disillusioned reading Lenin's *Materialism and Empirio-criticism*. Perhaps with him we will have the embryo of an Indian contemplative life. India, too, poses problems that are at present insoluble. From the grafting of Christianity into India I expect that the Church will be more deeply immersed in the heart of the Trinitarian Mystery, this divine *co-esse*, this *sun-on* and *sun-hen* (the 'communial', synontologic mystery) which must order from above the progress of our life and our thought.[20]

Wondering about the reason for this lack of vocations, Monchanin frequently said that they came either too soon or too late. The value of contemplation was not held in high esteem by the Indian Church. Two centuries of evangelization which had been focused almost exclusively on *pariahs* and the lower castes had created only works of mercy and social service, admirable as they are. This is understandable, given the destitution and misery of the farmers and the great masses of people crowded in urban areas. Men who hunger and suffer are not inclined toward supernatural realities other than through the witness of charity directed toward their basic needs. Furthermore, for converts to Christianity a type of contemplation sharing in the cultural traditions of India was still quite unthinkable. Christians had been repeatedly told that Hinduism was one of the faces of the Evil One and it was thus difficult for them to find it a way toward God. India itself was undergoing the intoxication, if not of Marxism, at least of what is efficient and what is immediate.

It must also be admitted that the austere life of the two priests could only serve to alienate even those friends, priests or religious, who were sympathetic with their ideas but who did not feel prompted to share their asceticism and their way of life. The climate was hot and humid; the huts which were thatched and open to all the inclemencies of the weather were scattered through a forest of mango-trees, infested with reptiles (at night one dared walk about only if armed with a stick to drive them off). The only furniture consisted of a cot and a few book shelves to preserve their books from termites. Indian food is highly seasoned and completely vegetarian. (Visitors, after their first stay, often brought their own food with them.) Threats of flooding at times obliged them to leave the *ashram* and hurriedly to seek refuge in a nearby town. A Carmelite once said to Father Monchanin, 'Your *ashram* is too miserable; you should imitate the poor not as they are but as they should be.'

'Such a maxim,' Monchanin later replied, 'is worthy of being penned by some twentieth century Provincial Friend![21] The Hindu *sannyāsis* go much farther in the emptying of self.' And he added with a touch of humor, 'I shall gladly consent to owning a bath [they bathed in the Kavery River] when every Indian family is equipped with one.'

It is thus understandable that the *ashram* never gave the appearance of being a foundation in the strict sense; at no time did the number of ashramites ever exceed six. This is not too surprising, if we think of the desert fathers, who for a long time lived in the solitary places of Egypt and Palestine, and, beginning in the fifth century, disappeared in the desert, their spiritual heritage being perpetuated, especially in the West, by monasteries that were more formally structured. But unlike these ancient anchorites, Father Monchanin never cut himself off from human contacts, and he always accepted any type of apostolate that was suggested to him. In addition to preaching retreats for priests, nuns, and seminary students and also replacing village pastors, he often participated in philosophical and religious conferences and in meetings of indologists. His Greek turn of mind, his great dislike of proselytism, had prepared him to be a man of dialogue.

In January, 1953, at Pondicherry he gave a lecture on the theology of time in which he adopted the ideas of Dom Casel. In July of the same year he was at Tiruvannamalai with Father Le Saux.

> We spent six weeks there exploring Hinduism which gave freely the best of itself—pure *advaita*—in contact with and in memory of the great wise holy man, Ramana Mahārshi. We both had the feeling of living a golden legend, in which the perceived and the imagined are indistinguishable, and of sometimes approaching an experience, a transcendental understanding, which completely

escapes images, concepts, norms. Pure mysticism
that disappears like the lines of the horizon before
the scientist. The way that the most philosophical
of them put it into conceptual terms is quite disappointing. There are many flagrant contra-
dictions—the ideal of *māyā* is an intellectual
monster.

On Pentecost, 1955, he was asked to speak on Christian
mysticism to the Congress of Religions at Bangalore. He
wrote the following summary of his impressions:

We (a recently arrived English Benedictine and
myself) were the only two Catholics there.[22] There
were more Protestants, a few Muslims, Buddhists,
Jains, and Zoroastrians (Parsis). The majority
were Hindu. The atmosphere was friendly. But
there were too many theosophists (they are people
who spread obscurity and confusion by combining
all religions). A professor from the University of
Madras, a pure Hindu (*advaitin*), was the
outstanding person at the congress. The overall
tendency: common front of religions against the
invasion of materialism and atheism.

My paper (only twenty minutes long) seemed to
provide the chairman with new philosophical ideas.
He as asked me to develop this same theme (Col
2:9, the concept of God and the justification of
Christian *apophatism* at the philosophical congress
in Nagpur in December).

The following year at Pondicherry he gave yet another
lecture, on Teilhard de Chardin, the man, the scientist, the
thinker, the believer. He had known him in Paris and had
corresponded with him. With only slight qualification, he had
the greatest admiration for Teilhard's work. As a member of
the *Group lyonnais d'études médicales, philosophiques et
biologiques*, he had once given a rather Teilhardian talk

entitled: 'Forms, Life, and Thought.'[23] The concluding part
of this talk reveals their agreement on the very highest level,
that of thought and spiritual life.[24]

> In short, if it is true that matter is for life, and life
> for the spirit, and the spirit for Christ, and Christ
> for God, must we not also say that the structures
> of matter and of life and of human values have but
> one meaning, that of being stages and signs of this
> definite rhythm, which is the movement, the
> return to God of all that God has made, the extasis
> of humanity, the spirit of the earth?

In a letter written to his mother in the beginning of 1957
on the feast of Saint Paul the Hermit (15 January) he
mentioned the various meetings in which he had taken part:

> My life in December was the opposite of a
> hermit's life—very busy. First, the Catholic Study
> Week at Madras.[25] Nearly two hundred delegates
> from all over India studied together some of the
> problems of adaptation and culture, Christian art
> in India, Catholic Action, etc. I spoke on the
> Quest of the Absolute according to Hinduism and
> Christianity.[26]

> Then ten days at Pondicherry. At the Institute I
> gave a lecture on the Dead-Sea Scrolls and the
> origins of Christianity.

> Finally the Congress of Religions at Madras. We
> were deluged with talks on Hindu, Moslem,
> Buddhist, Jain, and even Christian saints. I spoke
> on Saint John of the Cross. Including myself,
> there were five Catholic priests. A warm, friendly
> atmosphere and deep spiritual conversations. I
> heard a concert of excellent Indian music
> performed by a blind violinist, and I saw some
> classical dance recitals—which are always so
> beautiful!

Commenting on the Madras Congress, a newspaperman wrote:

> It is impossible to analyze the different relationships. Suffice it to say that a deep impression was made on the audience by Father Monchanin, whose talk ranged from the depths of the Vedanta to the heights of Trinitarian mysticism, and by Dom Griffiths who opened up new avenues of comparison between Hinduism and the Christian mystery. [27]

But he was happiest to be at the Institute in Pondicherry where he could continue his research into Indian culture. He had many faithful friends there—both Indians and Europeans —with whom he felt a deep rapport whatever their religious beliefs may have been. These were stimulating visits for Father Monchanin. His contacts with Hindus and his reading of sacred texts brought him in touch with eternal India, and he often wondered whether India was turning its back on its glorious past under the impact of technical civilization and the materialistic ideologies of the West.

On the feast of the Epiphany, he wrote of his hopes for another institute on the same intellectual level, where Christian scholars would examine the cultural and religious traditions of India in order to discover the ways by which Christianity could penetrate it. It was a dream which he had entertained since coming to India and which would always be with him through years of reflection and prayer.

> I am very fond of this feast of the Epiphany: the Wisemen, the symbols of peoples who have not yet known the light of Christ but who walk in search of it, in the glimmer of visible things—like India which has for thousands of years been making the difficult pilgrimage to truth and holiness and which does not tire of being directed toward the 'Unknown God', the one who is not known when he is known and who is known when he is not known.

We must pray for a center of advanced studies and research where priests and laymen might meet to further their knowledge of the languages, philosophies and religions of India, in order to penetrate them—into their very substance—with Christianity. India must be rethought in terms of Christianity, and Christianity in terms of India, as was done previously in Greece. Great visions of the future which my mortal eyes will not see perhaps, like Moses who died before he reached the Promised Land but who was consoled because his people would enter it after him.

His long stay in India, his continually deepening knowledge of religious thought and his contacts with men of many cultures and social classes had enabled Father Monchanin to evaluate carefully the obstacles to conversion. In 1951 he wrote frankly to his friend, Dr René Biot:

Since we lead a life that is withdrawn, we have been able to have spiritual contact with Hindus whom we would never have met otherwise. That does not mean, of course, that they are ready for conversion. The more I am with them, the larger the gulf seems that separates us—us Christians and not us Europeans—from them. They have no sense of uneasiness. At least no uneasiness concerning *their* religion. Some of them—the better, the more humble—feel they are very far from their own ideal. But they never attribute their spiritual limitations to their doctrine or discipline. They love and venerate Christ and rank him among the very great. But they refuse to grant him a unique position. They adore God whether in the universe, which they readily identify with his manifestations, the most exterior part of himself, or more generally within their inner being, like the hidden Norm, the Itself of their myself. The personality of God seems to them merely an anthropomorphic

representation to go beyond. In the same way, the
personality of man seems to them metaphysically
linked to the egoism they readily accept—even
desire—the prospect of their own disappearance as
distinct consciousness, a disappearance which in
their eyes conditions their identification with
infinite Consciousness which admits no further
distinctions, being utter Simplicity. All that a
Christian can do is to attempt to be a witness to
Christ among them and to prepare from afar his
coming in the same way as John the Baptist.

This opinion was not based on fleeting impressions. The
passage of years merely confirmed it. Father Monchanin
constantly encountered the difficulty of eliciting among cultivated Indians, even those with whom he felt some degree of
spiritual harmony, a curiosity about their own faith or of
arousing among them the desire to know the highest truths of
Christianity. His correspondence and notes reveal with much
sensitivity his suffering in the face of the 'wall of separation'
between him and those for whose salvation he had devoted
his life and accepted total renunciation.

We find among Hindus a similar belief and lack of
knowledge about Christianity. They are convinced
that their religion is the highest form of the
sacred. The more religious they are, the farther
they are from Christ. They understand meditation
more easily than vocal prayer or sacraments, and it
is in their heart that they find God. Yet, they have
great reverence for Jesus Christ in whom they see
a supreme manifestation of God. They are not at
all attracted by the Church (the human, all too
evident, conceals the divine from them). Conversion is abhorrent to them: it seems a betrayal,
cowardice.

Christianity, a religion of time, of history, of the
Incarnation, seems to them to be imperfect

wisdom. In this sense, contrary to Einstein and Spinoza, they turn their backs on the universe.

The uneducated do not think about this at any length and are happy to follow their customs. For them, all religions are equal: 'Different paths toward God like rivers which lose themselves in the sea.'

I too feel my own ineffectiveness. Hindus aware of their Hinduism, and especially Brahmans, have no sense of religious uneasiness. They live in a closed system, although its contours are shifting and although they remain open to the infinite— and there they find their spiritual food. I have no idea how the Gospel of the one and unique Christ (which they find extravagant) can reach them. The holier they are the farther they are from it.

The lack of spiritual uneasiness in the typical Hindu is doubtless the most difficult trial for any Westerner to face. We would prefer almost any other form of despair.

A few months before his death he wrote again:

The root of the matter is that Hindus are not spiritually uneasy. They believe they possess supreme wisdom and thus how could they attach any importance to the fluctuations or investigations of those who possess lesser wisdom. Christ is *one* among *avatāras*. Christianity in their eyes is a perfect moral doctrine, but a metaphysics which stops on the threshold of the ultimate metamorphosis.

From these and other quotations, we must not infer an admission of failure. Father Monchanin's lucid mind never diminished his sense of charity or his hope. On the contrary, according to him, charity and hope demand an increasing awareness of the differences between Christianity and Hinduism. The encounter between them—if it were possible—would come about only in reciprocal truthfulness. Shortly after the founding of the *ashram* he said to an Indian friend:

> Is our *Shantivanam* worthy of its name, 'Grove of Peace?' I would like it to be. I don't think we should over-emphasize or underemphasize the divergences between Hindus and Christians. But aren't these divergences themselves really incentives: an appeal to both sides to put fully into practice that which we consider to be the essence of our *dharma*? What I would like to see prevail among Christians and Hindus is not mutual ignorance and scorn, or facile syncretism which smoothes down rough edges and reduces everything to a rather empty moralism, but instead a real philosophical emulation and especially an emulation of holiness.

The search for ways that Christian thought might penetrate Indian thought and for ways through which Indians might reach the truth of Christianity was a long and painful one. And if, in the end, he recognized that it was almost impossible—humanly—never in his innermost being did he despair of the salvation of India. The crisis which both Hinduism and Christianity were undergoing at the time did not shake his faith in 'the advent—on the eschatological horizon—of Christ clothed in the glory of India like a *Chakravartin*, having assumed the values of India, values purified, unified and trans-essenced in himself.'[28]

> This is India's Advent. Conversions are rare. Public opinion is against them. It would perhaps be better if they were even rarer still. If I were to judge according to the examples of conversions

which I have seen at close range, most of them are
inspired by self-interest. Such 'rice-Christians', as
they are called, are an obstacle to the conversion
of those who are concerned with the problem of
religion. A large part of the young are slipping
toward agnosticism and indifference. One might
almost say that our attempt to rethink Hinduism in
Christ comes too late. Hinduism already is split
apart. *We must all the same and even 'hoping
against hope' believe in India and timeless China
and prepare their transmutation.*

This was his unshakeable hope which was sustained in
charity. Monchanin loved India, humanly and religiously,
with a fervent and unstinting love. This land was truly his
chosen land, the Indian people his people—'his mother, his
brother, and his sisters' (Matt 12:50). With deep respect, he
loved them equally in their greatness and in their misery. For
long years, and to the very limit of his strength, he attempted
to espouse the conditions of their life and to share their hopes
and sufferings. And nothing—lack of understanding, disappointments, failures—could make him turn away from
them. Rarely in the history of missions does one find such a
strong willingness for incorporation and assimilation. Finally,
in regard to the spiritual future of India, he believed in the
power of Love, the love which accepts everything, understands everything, is silent and transfigures. That was his
conclusion to his lecture on the Quest of the Absolute, the
ultimate expression of his thought. After having noted without minimizing it, the gulf which separates Indian mysticism
and Christian mysticism, he wrote:

> Meanwhile, our task is to keep all doors open, to
> wait with patience and theological hope for the
> hour of the advent of India into the Church, in
> order to realize the fullness of the Church and the
> fullness of India. In this age-long vigil, let us
> remember that very often *amor intrat ubi intel-*

lectus stat ad ostium: Love can enter where the intellect must stand at the door.

> *The smallest effort to graft*
> *the depths of Christianity*
> *into the depths of India.*

It was in this way that Father Monchanin spoke of the *ashram* to an Indian friend in 1954. Indeed from the exterior, the *ashram* did not seem to have lived up to the expectations of its founders. After five years the number of members in the community was extremely small and several of them, after a period of trial, left the *ashram* to follow their own way. Noting that *Shantivanam* did not develop as he had hoped and noting, too, that he seemed to be marking time, he said sadly, 'Our hopes haven't materialized; we are at a critical stage.'

But the extent of his spiritual influence cannot be measured by visible signs. The story of the *ashram*, like that of his life, is an interior one. Few religious centers in India or elsewhere received as many and as varied a number of visitors: newspapermen, civil servants, politicians, professors, personal friends, priests and religious, Hinduized Westerners and Indian ascetics (these latter often staying for weeks), Indologists, Christians from the nearby village of Kulitalai. Some came out of curiosity and others (by far the more numerous), drawn by the deeply spiritual atmosphere that prevailed, came in search of comfort or advice. Father Monchanin's deepest apostolic work was precisely in these encounters and the long conversations which he had with his guests. What people have said about him, even in India, and from personal letters written to him, it is clear that for many he was a 'path to God'.

Having returned from India, a number of these guests spoke and wrote of the *ashram* as a highly spiritual place and of Monchanin himself in terms which offended his sense of humility. He was upset by this and frequently complained of the publicity he received:

Without my knowledge my name has become a
sort of myth. I am beginning to be annoyed by so
many articles about a work which at present is
merely a hope. Like the worker-priests, what we
need is silence.

The story of *ashram* is, as we have said, an inner one. In
point of fact, the last two years did not bring about any
change in the life of the small community. The only note-
worthy event was the arrival of Father Dharma, an Indian
priest from Tiruchirapalli. ('I am giving you one of my best
priests,' the Bishop had written to Monchanin.)   Shortly
afterward Monchanin met Msgr. MacGregorios during a trip
to the South, and he thought briefly of moving into the
diocese of Trivandrum. He wrote to Father Le Saux:

The prospect of the Syrian rite has many advantages: an understanding archbishop, the possibility of a vernacular liturgy, and doubtless a
better source of vocations. We must carefully
study these advantages without making any
commitment. I would prefer the formula: an
ashram located at the intersection of a Hindu
country and a Christian country, a sort of bridge
between two spiritual worlds. Keep studying the
prospects in Malayalam-speaking regions.

In the margin of this letter he added:

It is no slight matter to become familiar with these
two languages (Syriac and Malayalam); all the
more because it is also question of a liturgical,
historical, patristic initiation. Father Mahieu seems
to have a liking for this semitic world. Perhaps he
will be the founder of the Syriac *Shantivanam.*[29]

This plan was never put into effect and the hoped for reorientation did not come about. Father Dharma, who was a
man of action, was very upset by *Shantivanam's* lack of

influence. 'You are burying your ideal,' he said to Father Monchanin, and he began plans to move the *ashram* to Kulitalai or Tiruchirapalli, to the very midst of a noisy city, thinking that it would be there that they would have spiritual contacts—with Protestants, it is true, more than with Hindus. Without being strictly opposed to this plan, Father Monchanin preferred his location and his role as quiet witness and hermit.

Due to the as yet uncertain and indefinite state of *Shantivanam*, he tended more and more to believe that he would never see with his eyes of flesh the advent of that Indian monasticism which had been the goal of his foundation:

> The *ashram* will probably be a failure. Others who
> will be more worthy will take up the task again.
> Let us pray for the coming of Indian monks. We
> shall stand aside, and they will bring into reality
> that which is for us merely a dream. And let us
> wait in hope and unalterable patience—hope, the
> most difficult virtue that the Spirit gives.

Such was the state of the *ashram* in the spring of 1957. Father Monchanin had only a few more months to live. Although he seemed interiorly youthful, he felt himself growing old, and complained that he no longer had the same powers of concentration. Frequently he experienced great fatigue. From the tone of his correspondence (although he confided less and less often in his friends) and from the growing number of allusions to his childhood and youth, it would seem that he had a presentiment of his approaching death. His real thoughts and feelings were most apparent in letters to his mother, who was at that time very old and who had long been bedridden as a result of an accident. She was to survive him by a month.

Shantivanam-Kulitalai, 18 February 1957

Dearest Mother,
　　　　I thought of you very much and said my Mass

for you on 29 January. Your eighty-ninth spring-time! A scandalous age to live to, you say. The spirit has no age!

On 2 February, I thought of a Candlemas Day long ago when I was about eighteen. The three of us, you, Nina,[30] and I went on a pilgrimage to Chiroubles. The weather was beautiful, cold and dry. A long time ago!

On another Candlemas Day, in Belgium, my last winter in Europe. Mass at the Benedictine abbey of Mont-Cesar, at Louvain, and then leaving for Paris. A pale yellow light under a pale sun. You are no longer making earthly journeys—nor will I ever again. I move in a confined circle: Madras, Bangalore, Trivandrum, Pondicherry are the far-thest places I go. You, a prisoner in your bed.

World news now reaches me only after being fil-tered through space and time—and thus muted—and it is better that way. No daily newspapers. Two weeklies (the Belgian edition of *Témoignage Chrétien* and *Le Monde*) are sent to me. It takes about two months for them to get here—a long detour around Africa, since Suez is blocked. In that way I see events in retrospect, which is more fitting for a philosopher! Let's repeat with Spinoza: 'We feel and we experience that we are eternal,' and let's see things, if not *sub specie aeterni*, at least from the point of view of Sirius.

I can see you surrounded by your grandchildren and great-grandchildren. A geometrical progres-sion! That was the earthly blessing promised to the patriarchs—unto the fourth and fifth genera-tion. Hope rises with life.

You give everyone a splendid example of patience and quiet courage. Old age is beautiful when it culminates in serenity.

I think about you very often, and about the
'plundered gardens of childhood'.

With love,
Jules

A photograph taken at this time on the banks of the
Kavery River reveals that the shadow of death was already
upon him. In June he received an invitation from friends in
Bangalore which he was forced to turn down. He wrote the
following apology:

My health has declined considerably in the past
three months. My liver is causing pain, no appe-
tite, constant fatigue. A month ago at Pondicherry
I had a series of medical tests. Nothing serious
was detected, but I am in a state of depression.
Yet inwardly I am at peace.

In July other friends took him to a mountain resort at
Kodai. He remained there several weeks, enjoying the
natural beauty, surrounded by fine books. The trip was one
of his last earthly pleasures. A further medical examination
at Pondicherry revealed, in addition to some minor ailments,
a tumor located near the stomach. Finding that the hospital
did not possess the necessary equipment or blood for trans-
fusions, his doctor told him he would have to leave as soon as
possible for Paris, where the risks of the operation would be
far less. As agonizing as it was for Father Monchanin to be
uprooted from India and his work, he agreed, on the
condition that he would obtain his return visa. He left India
by plane from Bombay, where Father Le Saux, returning from
the Himalayas, had waited for him. And when he reached
Paris, he was entrusted to eminent specialists at the Hospital
of Saint-Antoine.

During his last days, he was surrounded by old and dear

friends. Unmindful of his own suffering, he greeted everyone
with his usual radiant, warm smile, showing concern about
each person's problems, resuming conversations which had
been interrupted by years of separation. Truly he gave fully
of what he had received from God. In his emaciated body,
his mind remained as keen as before, his glance penetrating
and luminous, embracing both persons and things with
love.... He spoke about everything, art, science, philosophy,
mysticism, according to the interests of his visitors, and frequently his words were marked with humor. But his thought,
like his prayer, returned time and again to the mystery of the
Trinity, which he had contemplated for so long and which had
been the great passion of his life. Although very near death,
he still found the strength to dictate some notes on the
Trinity.[31]

The operation, which had at first been delayed, finally
revealed that his ailment was incurable. He accepted his
sacrifice lucidly and serenely—offering his life for his friends,
India, the Church, for the glory of the Trinity.

On the morning of his eternal union with God, 10 October,
having received Communion, he became silent, stretched out
his arms in a cross in a final gesture of oblation, and after a
few hours quietly died.

At his funeral, which was held in the church of Saint-
Severin in Paris, the presence of so many friends, priests,
religious, laity of every race and belief prefigured the
catholicity in Love to which he had dedicated himself.

His body now lies in the cemetery of Bièvres, a small
village outside of Paris which he loved for its beauty. It was
at Bièvres that his closest friends had welcomed him back to
France. Engraved on the tombstone are the Benedictine
cross which he wore, his French and Indian names, two dates
and his title of priest, the only one to which he was
attached.[32]

> What I wish for is the Absolute (I mean a
> participation in the Absolute) in truth and Its

truth, even if no intellectual construct is linked to it—although I find it difficult to breathe in too pure an atmosphere where ideas cannot be crystalized. The God of mysticism is beyond all feeling, all hope, in the burning solitude where he reflects himself and unifies himself. It is because of the mystery of the Trinity—Alpha and Omega— that I am a Christian.

Such a desire for communion with the Absolute—the Trinitarian God—was basically to Father Monchanin 'the magnetizing pole of thought and the unifying center of life'.[33]   But his quest for the Absolute was never a solitary search, or his contemplation cut off from humanity.   India, more particularly, was the place where his love of God and of men was manifested.   Although he deeply loved the land of his vocation and the people with whom he had identified himself, his prayer overreached time and space and was always universal in dimension.   This universality became for him the law of all Christian life.   He once wrote to Sister Marie Abraham, one of his spiritual daughters serving Christ in Islam:

Dilate the Church.   We each have our unique place.   The highest parts of this Body are the most irreplaceable.   Dilate the Church by your prayer. Never will it be the prayer of a person in isolation. It will be a prayer as open as Christ's arms on the cross, as vast as the Redemption.   You will have the restlessness of the world to save—constant intercession for the union of Christians.   For the world to believe that God sent his Word, his disciples must appear united.   Restlessness of those who do not believe in the One Mediator, who have kept to the belief in the God of Abraham—the restlessness of Israel, the restlessness of Islam, and of the remainder of the world: China so ready to grasp all the resonances of the Incarnation; India thirsting for contemplation; primitive peoples unaware of the obstacle we know so well, the over analytic mind—and for that portion of humanity which has rejected God and the battle. In this way, your prayer will be catholic, and fully so.

Before leaving Europe he had earlier written to Louis Massignon:

Even if we had converted everyone living in the whole world in order to make them Christians in our very inadequate image, there would still be all the dead of India for me and of Islam for you. As long as we have not embraced that powerful inter-cession for all the dead which alone will allow for the convergence of different human groups, from their origins to the Judge of the Last Judgment, Christ with his hands pierced by his justice, we will not have fulfilled the vocation that God has written in our hearts, a universal vocation.[34]

From this point of view his attempt at Indian monasticism did not exhaust the wealth of his apostolate and spiritual experience. The great problems facing the Church today— ecumenism, incarnation and presence in the world, priesthood of the laity, meeting of cultures, dialogue between believers and non-believers—did not cease to fill his thought and determine his actions.

The failure of his mission, in human terms, he accepted as proof of its ultimate fruitfulness. Unless the seed die.... 'We are only arrows pointing the way,' he often said. And humbly he wanted nothing but that. But the role of pioneers is to open up new paths toward eternal realities. He realized his vocation in a death which was not sterility but parturition. It is his life which is ultimately his essential message. And through death he remains near to every person, teaching us to 'resolve these paradoxes: being together and being alone, love of the world and asceticism of the spirit, the taste of the earth and the savor of eternity'.[35]

FOOTNOTES

1. Jules Monchanin and Henri Le Saux, *A Benedictine Ashram*, Rev. ed. (Douglas, 1964) p. 10.

2. J. Monchanin and H. Le Saux, *Ermites du Saccidānanda* (Tournai-Paris, 1957).

3. *Ermites du Saccidānanda*, pp. 21-22.

4. *A Benedictine Ashram*, pp. 10-11.

5. *Ibid.*, p. 13.

6. *Ibid.*

7. *Ibid.*, pp. 13-14. See also p. 14, note 4: '*Theandric:* of Christ, as God-man, i.e. perfect God and perfect man. *Pleroma:* one of the deepest and most difficult words in the vocabulary of Saint Paul, especially in the Epistles to the Ephesians and Colossians. It means *fullness* (plenitude, *plenum*) and conveys a manifold meaning: 1) the plenitude of godhead by which Christ is consubstantial with God the Father (cf. Col 1:19, Col 2:9); 2) the plenitude of grace enjoyed by the humanity of Christ; 3) the plenitude that the Holy Church receives from Christ; 4) the "supplement" that the Church gives to Christ Himself as His Mystical Body, "the body, the fullness of Him (*Corpus ejus et plenitude ejus*) who fills all in all (Eph 1:23) "ever growing" "to perfect manhood", to the measure of the stature of the fullness of Christ (*in virum perfectum, in mensuram aetatis plenitudinis Christi*) (Eph 4:13)", cf. Col 1:24: "I [Paul] fill up that which is lacking in Christ's afflictions in my flesh for his body's sake, that is, the Church." '

8. *Ibid.*, pp. 14-15.

9. See: Brhad-Aranyaka-Upanishad, I, 3, 28.

10. *Ibid.*, p. 15.

11. *Ibid.*, p. 16.

12. *Ibid.*, pp. 16-17.

13. *Ibid.*, p. 17.

14. *Ibid.*, p. 17-18.

15. Madeleine Biardeau in *L'abbé Jules Monchanin*, p. 116.

16. Brahmo Śamāj was founded in 1828 by Rammohan Roy, to worship God as expounded in the *Vedānta*. This theistic movement, which was intellectual and strongly influenced by Western scientific, political, and religious thought, was active in opposing ancient traditions and sought a synthesis with Christianity. The Ramakrishna Mission, founded by disciples of the holy man Ramakrishna (1836-1886), is an order of monks holding that all forms of religion are valid ways to the Eternal, and is influential in Europe and America.

17. Ananda Coomaraswamy (1877-1947) an art historian born in Ceylon who is largely credited with having built up the great Far Eastern collection of the Museum of Fine Arts in Boston. He was the author of many books on Far Eastern art and culture.

18. 629-645 A.D.

19. Emperor 274-237 B.C.

20. The Latin term *co-esse* would emphasize the Trinitarian existence. Using Greek terms, Monchanin reveals what love there is in its unity (*sun-hen*) which he translates as 'communial' and what source of existence there is in *sun-on*, which he translates by synontologic.

21. Monchanin was referring to Pascal's satirical *Lettres Provinciales*, a series of eighteen satirical letters against the Jesuits written in the seventeenth century.

22. Dom Bede Griffiths.

23. See his concluding essay in *Formes, Vie et Pensée* (Lyons: Lavandier, 1930-31).

24. For a contrast as well as a comparison between Teilhard and Monchanin by one who knew them both very well, see Henri de Lubac, *Images de l'abbé Monchanin,* pp. 119-151.

25. All India Study Week, Madras, 6-13 December 1956. See: *Indian Culture and the Fullness of Christ* (Madras, 1957) which contains both the program and the principal lectures.

26. This speech, considered by de Lubac and others as the culmination of Monchanin's philosophical thought, appears below, pp. 127-132.

27. See the description in *Swami Parama Arubi Anandam* (Tiruchirapalli, 1959), pp. 42, 93.

28. 'Trans-essenced' means simultaneously that which transcends and also that which exceeds the essence, both as movement and as condition.

29. A monastic foundation inspired by Syriac spirituality, such as that at Kurisumala (South India).

30. His sister.

31. See below, p. 181, *The Trinity: An Essay in the Light of Personalism.*

32. A more detailed account of Monchanin's last days can be found in *L'abbé Jules Monchanin*, pp. 27-9.

33. *L'abbé Jules Monchanin*, p. 29.

34. Louis Massignon, *Opera minora*, ed. par Y. Moubarac, Vol. III (Dar Al-Maaref-Liban, 1963), p. 770.

35. Jean Lyon, 'Vie et mort de l'abbé Monchanin,' *Promesses* (Noel, 1961).

PART TWO
Selected Writings

NOTES

WHAT HAS ONCE BEEN, lives eternally, and nothing can change its having been. In heaven itself we shall remember the earth and its ephermeral and eternal joys, like that rose Claudel speaks of, which 'sensed once, is sensed all summer long.' Strange how very small things can thus acquire in our memory a density which is almost infinite.

Does the term *outdated* have any meaning? Neither Homer, nor Plato, nor the Bible have aged, and Dante's loves are as alive as in his own time. There is something eternal—much of the eternal, and more of the eternal than the transitory—in man.

The eternal is not escape from life but fullness of life.

Each presence is life-giving communion.

Beings, unfolding and maturing in the shadow of a being....

The capacity for presence increases with the capacity for recollection.

The union of two saints who do not know each other is far more real and intimate than the union of one branch with another from the same tree, fed from the same sap; incomparably more real and intimate than the union of people in the same city, of members of the same family, than the union of lovers when they are two in one same flesh, in a same identifying love; and still more real and even more one than the union of self with self, whether at the moment of *cogito*, when the in-itself and the for-itself coincide in a flash of intuition—or even at the moment of contemplation when *enstasis* is transformed into *extasis*. It is from the union of the Mystical Body that all other union flows. It is itself participation.

In the same way that there is 'inherence'[1] of each soul in 'Circumincession,'[2] there is a reciprocal interiority of souls. Space and time lose their hold on those who have felt their souls possessed by God.

Why do we desire 'transfiguration on this earth itself' when it is a myth? Whereas, above all we are promised something so much better: a most intimate union with the Living God—the Holy Trinity—so that its life becomes our life! 'God all in all,' Saint Paul puts it so beautifully.[3] That is all that counts. We must keep our eyes riveted on that glorious Parousia, which will transfigure the universe and our immortal bodies.

Mystery is the place of the soul, its sea.

Is it true that 'a man who renounces the world puts himself in a position to understand it'? True and false certainly. To renounce is to step back; thus there is a possibility of perspective. It can also mean to forget, to blaspheme something one doesn't share. Everything depends on the quality of renunciation: authentic or artificial. Authentic renunciation implies no insult to life. And as for the reasons people renounce life: there is renunciation which is cowardice, or flight, or escape, or even narcissism. There is a renunciation which is *extasis* in God. There is also simply waiting. A vigil, slow and gray like Advent, on the threshold of eternity.

One must renounce only what has been attained—for one can only go beyond what has been reached—only renounce fullness in view of a greater fullness. A beautiful *mantra* declares:

> *Fullness here on earth.*
> *Fullness beyond fullness.*
> *From fullness gathered comes fullness.*

God is not the *other*, the competitor jealous of our joys. He is *Totally-Other;* He is *Totally-Mine.* He is the fullness which sometimes occurs in our fullness, or most often in our emptiness.

Rites without soul are empty. But with faith their appearance is completely changed: they are bearers of the Spirit. In the splendid words of St John Chrysostom: If you were incorporeal (angelic) God would have given you incorporeal gifts; but since you are both of spirit and of flesh, God has enveloped the intelligible for you under the veil of the senses. And the Christmas Preface proclaims: 'So that through things seen we may be drawn to the love of things unseen.' This is the very logic of the Incarnation; at the same time it is a demand of our nature as incarnate spirit and members of a human society. The humility of the rite readies us for receiving greater gifts—and the greatest of all is the charisma of *agapè*—love of God and love of our brothers. If submission to an external order seems sometimes to restrict and imprison interior experience, it is only preparation for further dilation: an expansion which opens toward the infinite. God knows us and he loves us! And he wants to dilate us to his fullness.

God is Love. God is Beauty. And the reflections created by goodness and art fill us with yearning for his Absolute.

'The salt of the earth' (Matt 5:13). The Christian is the 'salt of the earth' by his oblation of the universe to the Creator. God never fails, even for a second, to be present to us. But we are blind and deaf to this presence, to this attraction, to this gift of ourselves in the inviolate solitude of our consciousness. Think less of sin and more of mercy. Pure adoration is what purifies.

Beyond books there is prayer. There is silence before God. There is God who calls us. To pray is not enough. The world has been saved, not by the proclamation of the Beatitudes, but by the Cross, nakedness, helplessness, death. In this I can understand all the saints: Andrew, Ignatius, Francis of Assisi, Theresa, John of the Cross. Suffering is configuration to the mystery of Christ: *Tristitia vestra vertetur in gaudium* (Your sorrow will be turned in joy—John 16:20). Paschal joy is the sorrow of Good Friday itself, transfigured from within, 'transubstantiated'. This is the testimony the world awaits: this Paschal joy which is transfigured sorrow.

Compensation is the essential law of the spiritual life. All suffering is a parturition. All suffering which seems meaningless in an individual person takes on absolute meaning in the suffering of Christ.

'God is the place of spirits, just as space is the place of bodies.' In him, there is neither absence nor distance.

It is when hope seems obliterated that despair takes hold of you. You question. Then you must be stretched out on the cross to relive this mystery of death, even if from this side of life you might not see the other side. You must retain an eschatological hope, be one with the stretching out of the Church, even when everything seems to fail—when you are stripped of everything, when everything is taken from you and torn out of you.

The meaning of life can be understood only at the moment of death, if it is conscious.

Love inscribes in the flesh a metaphysical thirst for the other. It breaks the ring of solitude of the monad enclosed in its *ipseity*. By its very presence, love rejects the desolate vision of the melancholy thinker who projects on consciousness the incommunicability characteristic of his own enclosed consciousness. The other, chosen, contemplated, loved in his very *alterity*, in his essential mystery, becomes the pole, the force of attraction. This communion without fusion, communion that, instead, sharpens differences and completes the identity of each person according to his own axis, always threatened and continually overcoming the monotony and confusion of daily life, growing deeper as it is spiritualized with the passage to time: this is the miracle of love. Transposed from one's spouse to God: this is the miracle of holiness.

The spirit of the Gospel must be reflected within the most resistant part of the temporal, that is, in the material world which is the zone of the unconverted. Personal charity is not enough.

When you begin with the tangible you end with the tangible. The spirit of the Gospel must be made to penetrate the tangible. It must be divine love which leads us to the search for our most distant brothers. But this has to be an exchange, otherwise there will not be love, for love is not in just one direction.

Keep bright the flame of thought and love: they are the same. Communicate around you this desire to understand and to give (and also to receive). There are too many enclosed minds.

ON SIMONE WEIL

About her writings there has been much controversy. Without any doubt she was a great woman, a soul seized by God. She seems to have been marked by a mysterious sign for her mission: 'At the intersection of the world of belief and the world of unbelief.' Nor did Moses himself enter the Land of Promise. Her demand for absolute sincerity compelled her to make a severe evaluation of her own life. She opens a way—or rather she moves along a way, opened before her by the Greek Fathers and even before them by Plotinus—of purification of the belief in God by a kind of 'atheism.' This is, if I understand it correctly, that negative theology (apophatism) of the kind that Bulgakov pursued so wisely himself (with a balance and with nuances that Simone, who died too young, had not yet been able to find). What is disconcerting about her is rather her *antisemitism on the religious level*, which recalls in an unpleasant way Marcion, his lack of historical perspective and his extreme affinity for the esoteric. This deviation—there is no other word for it—is most evident in her later notebooks (*Supernatural Knowledge*). Even so, she is one of God's gifts in our tragic times.

Complacency in pessimism is the temptation of our time: the 'novel of despair', 'literature of derision', existentialism focusing on nothingness, and 'dialectical theology'. In Origen's time it was more luminous. Dante didn't blaspheme life!

The preconception of perpetual involvement hardly serves as a satisfactory criterion—especially in theology. However sacred time is, eternity still overshadows it.

To endure is all that is possible in the present time, in this shattered world where we are condemned to live. People who talk with so much assurance about the 'sense of history' are lucky. How can we know the sense of history, even the most recent? It is revealed only in retrospect. Aren't those who 'make history' merely blind actors? It should be enough for us to know that we are where God has placed us to do an infinitesmal, ant-like task of unknown dimensions. It is the hour of the night of Gethsemane, the hour of silent offering, and thus the hour of hope: God alone. Faceless, unknown, unable to be perceived, yet unable to be rejected: God.

Hidden China and hidden India. Contemplation alone reaches them. I see India not in the image of the desert, nor of the sea, nor of the garden, but of the *cave*. Deeper, darker, flashes in a stark symbol. Passage: through the within to the beyond.

It is in the inviolate sanctuary of the contemplating mind that the encounter between India and Christianity will occur.

Like a cloud, India dims, sometimes abolishes, awareness of time.

It seems to me more and more doubtful that the essence of Christianity can be found by going through *advaita* (the non-dualism of Śankara).[4] *Advaita*, like *yoga* and more than *yoga*, is an abyss. Whoever dizzily plunges into it cannot know what he will find in its depths. I fear it may be *himself* rather than the living, triune God.

Indian holiness, like Indian art, will discover its own ways, once the Indian people, steeped in their civilization, fully live their Christianity. Otherwise it will be only an artificial construct.

It may be rash to ask Christians to rethink one of the fundamental mysteries of their faith, the Trinity or the Creation, without offering them a theology or a philosophy which is as coherent and as solid as the one implicitly criticized. But how else can we proceed? Greek, patristic, Latin, or medieval theology were not the construct of one man alone. How else can we proceed except by means of uncertain, faltering steps? Indian alone will, one day, give *her* theololgy to the heart of theology.

India needs places of silence and Christian meditation.

Can *yoga* be christianized? Today it is almost always associated with pelagianism, virtual atheism, and questionable *tantric* practices. Are the results really worth the price?

There is no room for grace in strict *yoga*, nor is there room, logically, for God. It is narcissism without Narcissus (its accidents, non-differential, being absorbed by its essence).

Our *ashram*: an image foreshadowing the totality of India, totally transfigured in the dead and resurrected Christ and in the Spirit sent forth.

This image, this India lives in us—waiting for the time and the place of its incarnation *ludens—līlā—in orbe terrarum* (playing—*līlā*—over the surface of the earth; cf. Prov 8:31). Its horizons as vast as the sea, a sea bathed in light and flaming like the Christic *Chakra*: the wheel of cosmic and human becoming in space-time and the wheel of asceticism which undoes (the Cross) what evil (dispersion) has done. The *ashram* must, within India and for India, within the Church and for the universal Church, be the creator of *unity*, that unity begged for by the priestly prayer of Christ and identical with perfect interiority.

The problem of time is one that obsesses me. How can we understand the relation of time to eternity? A philosophy and a theology of time are one of the crying needs of our age.

Each Christmas is a gift of childhood. The mystery of the threefold Birth which Tauler contemplated.[5] The temporal Birth defines time and history, leads toward the Eternal Birth and brings about the Internal Birth. The three activities are one: the unity of the Word, hidden in the Father, made manifest to the world, living in each person; the unity of the

Trinity which by this Epiphany shines forth over and above creation.

Christ is the Sacrament: *Ut per visibilia ad invisibilium rapiamur* (that through things seen we may be drawn to things unseen—Christmas Preface). The Church, his Body, is—from Pentecost to the Parousia—the place where the spiritual becomes incarnate, where the historical becomes porous to the eternal. With points of condensation: the sacraments which, like stars, gravitate around *the Sacrament* —his Body resurrected in its inadmissible, trans-biological, and trans-historical mode, no longer an element of the universe, but transcending the universe and ordering it by conferring its meaning on it (like Malebranche's *numbering-number*). Such is, at any rate, my theology of the eucharistic sign, so real that it is reifying the world. I believe that it is in and through the Eucharist that matter in being transubstantiated acquires its essence which is to signify. A sign of presence: of the self to the self; of the other—as other—to the self; of the world to the self. This 'mysteric' vision magnifies matter more than any 'dialectical materialism' and is the foundation of cosmic poetry (the poetry of a Hölderlin or a Rilke) and historical poetry, of time as such (the poetry of a T. S. Eliot in the *Four Quartets*).

Prayer of silence: the *Adsum* (Here am I) of Abraham leaving his land and sacrificing Isaac; the *Fiat* (So be it) of Mary at the Annunciation; of Christ at Gethsemane; the response to God in a moment's time. Silence is beyond vocal prayer and even meditation itself: dialogue with God which has become so interior that there is nothing else to respond except *Amen*, the adhering and the acquiescing of the whole being to God. It is pure adoration in love and unconditioned abandonment to the One who knows us and who loves us more than we could ever love. The Holy Spirit—and he alone—is the source of such a prayer. And from him comes that peace which can be neither named nor compared.

The Spirit breathes where he wills...Master of unforeseeable gifts who knows all that we do not know, who is perpetual rejuvenation, formless and limitless tenderness: the Spirit, the Formless One, who is the Faceless One. The Spirit who does not beget. He is the final, terminal person, after whom comes no other.... Because he is the last of the Trinity, he receives everything from the other two. And because he is final he is the Unity of the Father and the Son, the completion of love, consummation. He draws what draws near to him, shapes it to himself, and gives it to Christ.

God is essentially Love: Gift of Self to Self. He is constituted in his Unity by the Gift itself....Any vision of the Trinity must be conceived of according to the circumincession: that by which each Person is constituted in his relationship to the two Others, by his movement toward the two Others. The Father is the father—constituted by his paternity.... Each Person is constituted by his relationship to the two Others.

God is God because he is Several. If God is gift within himself, he is also Gift for the Others, the Creator. He can communicate his Joy and his Life.

We are snatched, seized by the last divine Person, the One most toward the margin of the Trinity, the Spirit which draws us back and shapes us to Christ. And the Son, in his turn, draws us back to the depth of the Father.

CHRISTIANIZATION OF ORIENTAL CULTURES

THE CHRISTIANIZATION of non-western civilizations requires, intellectually, a threefold task:

A) Rethink Christianity, recapture it in its first outpouring, disassociating it by thought from the conceptual modalities in which it was incorporated into Mediterranean civilizations: Judeo-Christian religious movements, Greek intellectuality, Roman institutions; the synthesis completed at the end of the patristic age (fifth century, Saint Augustine), overthrown, then readopted and diversified by the Barbarians, becoming Gallo-Roman, Hispanic, Anglo-Saxon, Slavic, then Medieval (the dual Christendom: western and Byzantine), and finally, since the Renaissance and the Reformation, modern, that is, above all, individual.

B) Isolate the essence and the movement of the civilization to be Christianized by cutting it off as close as possible to its source. Search for the 'virgin point', if it exists; for its dialectic, whose design is precontained in a period of awakening, when everything was already given in its virtual form and when nothing was yet crystallized (period of creative plasticity). For the West, this would be Greek thought between Parmenides and Aristotle; for China, under the Chou dynasty between the I-Ching[6] and Chuang-tze; for India, between the Brahmanas and Buddhism; for Islam, between the Koran and El Hallaj.

C) Grafting: reinsert Christianity in its purity into the civilization in question, which itself has been rethought in its purity.

Critical Analysis of These Three Points

A) If we rely on history itself, which has given Christianity its configuration, and on the idea of the development of dogma, the first point is open to question. Would not the desire to return to the starting point deprive us of dogmatic and spiritual explanations?

We have perhaps over-estimated the intellectual and spiritual importance of development, which is in fact more analytic than creative. No medieval *Summa* and no critical history of dogmas can surpass or even reach the theology of Paul and John. But actually, in certain respects, by structuring a whole system down to the last detail or by taking stock of each element historically, we may risk deadening the very noetic impulse of the origins of Christianity. Of course radicalism in this first instance would be absurd—we don't cross off history—and heretical—we don't have the right to declare something uncertain which the Church has recently declared certain. But we can, of course, think that the theological synthesis for India, China, or Islam (and perhaps even the West) need not be constituted around dogmatic explanations—even if they are stripped (as much as possible) of their western modalities and reduced to dogma itself—and even less constituted around a construct of thought which is necessarily dependent on a civilization with a fixed structure, no matter if it were inspired like that of Origen, or Augustine, or Thomas Aquinas, but that the theological synthesis must be constituted around the infrangible nucleus of the revelation itself of biblical Judeo-Christianity. In the West this nucleus has gathered along the way all sorts of intellectual movements which have formed around it a kind of nebula (*gnosis*, the still diffuse speculations of the Apostolic Fathers and the Alexandrians...). Subsequently it became stabilized in intelligible configurations which resemble constellations: Origenism,   Augustinsm,   Scotism,   Thomism, Newmanism.   This same gravitational center will have to gather up from India a completely different type of nebular material from which the ages will draw out still other intelligible constellations. *Catholic unity* rests upon this gravitational center, and *catholicity* is this indefinite firmament.

B)   The analysis of different civilizations seems to reveal the existence of privileged periods in which a multiform creative activity prefigured future developments without being crystallized in any very stable form.   These were relatively brief periods, analogous to certain critical states of living beings: periods of mutation (Cf. Le Roy: *Les Origines humaines et le développment de l'intelligence*, the distinction between mutation and orthogenesis).   The grasp of these creative moments gives us simultaneously the *essence* and the *movement* of a civilization, that is, its *structure* and its *rhythm*:   a structure which will persist, but which will perhaps be masked under alluvions either coming from the exterior or arising from internal complexities; and a rhythm which can be slowed down, but which will retain its dominant characteristics. We must discover the fundamental categories of the spirit, their relationships, and even more their historial ramifications.

C)   A new spiritual reality can in fact be born only from the conjunction of generally labile elements—the bearers of future time—and with the interference of creative periods (analogy with living things).

Applications: Language (the question of liturgical language...), history, literature, sciences, philosophies, and religions....

Because such problems concerned Father Monchanin from the earliest part of his intellectual life, we have included below, from among his philosophical and theological writings, two dense and difficult passages on 'Time and the Eternal' and 'Creation.' Despite their brevity and their technicality, they constitute veritable syntheses which he never managed to develop any further in his writings because he gave first place to prayer and to a life of dedication. During his stay in India he continually returned to these same themes, maintaining that Indians would not reach a Christian vision of the world so long as they had not become aware of a living reality of the Eternal which, however, does not deny a sense of history.

In April, 1954 he wrote to Father Le Saux:

The absolute freedom of the act of creation, free from all Greek necessarisim or Hindu *parināma* is an essential point. The Divine Essence cannot be affected by any connexity with the creature—even on the ideal level of dialectical moments. To put it more exactly, dialectical moments connote in God not existence but essence, in so far as we distinguish them in our way of thinking. (The Cabala and Jacob Boehme made use of them and yet were not free of pantheism.) The irreplaceable value of time, even for eternity, is for me another point of prime importance.... Such investigations, although necessary, require a serenity of spirit which is difficult to attain at this moment in the life of the Church when time and eternity seem disjointed.

In January, 1955, the following year, he wrote:

It is creation which must be rethought or rather resituated in the light of the revealed Christian mystery. In this mystery, Hinduism (and especially *advaita*) must die to be resurrected as Christian.

Any theory which is not sufficiently aware of this necessity constitutes a lack of fidelity both toward Christianity—we cannot mutilate it by separating it from its essence—and toward Hinduism—we cannot hide its fundamental error and its essential divergence in terms of Christianity. Hinduism must reject its *atman-brahman* equation, if it is to enter into Christ.

THE QUEST OF THE ABSOLUTE *

A HINDU SEEKER after the Absolute undertakes a longer journey than that of the Christian. The realization may last not only a lifetime but through a *lakh* or even a *crore* of lives.[7] The law of *Karma* and its consequence—innumerable rebirths and redeaths—are considered by every sect or school of Hinduism as both axiomatic and revealed truths.

Several ways are open to the Hindu seeker: the *Karmamārga*, the *Bhaktimārga*, and the *Jñānamārga*. The *Karmamārga* is the way of purely disinterested moral action, accomplished for the sake of *Dharma* (duty), without any regard for a reward, either in this world or in the world to come; it is the *niskāma Karmayoga* taught by Krishna to Arjuna in the immortal poem, the *Bhagavadgītā*. The *Bhaktimārga* is the way of devotion and love, of complete surrender and self-dedication to any *istadevatā* (chosen deity) or to one of the *avatāras* or even to a *guru*. It leads to perfection most Hindus thirsting after salvation. Let us mention only the two Schools of *Bhakti* of South India: the *Ālvārs* for Vaisnavism, and *Mānikka Vāsagar, Tāyumānavar, Rāmalinga Swāmigal*, etc. for Saivism; in Maharashtra, *Tukaram;* and, in North India, Tulsidās, Chaitanya and Kabir. The *Jñānamārga*, or the way of spiritual knowledge, is open

*Published originally in *Indian Culture and the Fullness of Christ* by The Catholic Centre of Madras. Text revised.

to those who recognize the Absolute in, through, or beyond every phenomenon. This is par excellence the way of the *Upanishads*, of the *Brahmasūtras* of Badarayana, of Gaudapada and of Sankaracarya. Since this last way is the one most removed, at least at first glance, from Christianity, it might be worth considering it more in detail.

First, the *Jñānamārga* does not exclude, but rather presupposes the accomplishment of *ṛta* (ritual duty) and *dharma* (moral duty). The first *śloka* of the *Brahmasūtras* runs as follows: *athāto brahmajijñāsā*, the quest of the Absolute (or literally 'the desire to know the Absolute'). *Athāto* has been interpreted in many ways. It may be quite well understood as the connection between the *Pūrvamīmāmsā* (a first exegesis, concerning the post-vedic ritualism) and the *Uttaramīmāmsā* (a second exegesis, the philosophical one). In fact, Śankara never denied the everlasting value of the immemorial religious tradition, and his philosophy, even in its most abstract aspects, is subservient to the *apauruseya śruti* (superhuman revelation). Yet, neither the *ṛta* nor the *dharma* is final. Both are to be transcended by one act of total renunciation: *sannyāsa*. The *sannyāsi* rejects, once and for all, everything mundane, and dedicates himself to the quest of the Absolute. Hereafter, *Brahman* is all in all for him. His *sādhana* (method of perfection) is the uninterrupted meditation (*Jñāna*) focused on *nirguna Brahman* (the unqualified Absolute in its absoluteness). The highest stage is the *jīvanmukti* in which the already liberated being, although still living in his body, is established on a plane beyond good and evil, and becomes undistinguishable from the eternal One. The ultimate liberation (*mokśa*) is twofold: in its negative aspect, it means the liberation from the *karma*, the release from the dreadful cycle of *samsāra* (called *mahābhaya*: the great terror in the *Bhagavadgītā*); in its positive aspect, it means *sahaja sthiti* (the stage of unborn-ness), the recognition of the ultimate changeless identity of the *jivātman*, the living soul, with *Brahman*. At this level, there is no more *samsāra*, nor *mokśa*; both are equally *māyā*, products of *avidyā* (ignorance). The unique *Brahman* in its unicity, in its *kaivalyatva* (ontological isolation), is the unique reality.

Such a mysticism is rightly qualified as apophatic (*apavāda*), negative as it is in its means and unspeakable and unthinkable as it is in its essence.

The Christian mystical approach to the Absolute is roughly divided into two main ways: the analogical one and the apophatic one. The analogical way starts from creatures and through them ascends step by step towards the living God. Is not every creature a reflection or a living image of the Creator? This path was followed by most of the mystics, and perhaps found its most sublime illustration in Saint Francis of Assisi as well as its theological justification in the marvelous spiritual treatise *Itinerarium mentis ad Deum*, written by Saint Bonaventure on the very Mount Alverno where his dear master had received, a few years before, the sacred stigmata. This ascension of the soul is in some way similar—with, of course, a very different philosophical and theological background—to the *Bhaktimārga* of the Hindus. It emphasizes the primacy of love over knowledge, and the Franciscan School of philosophy has maintained that primacy even on the plane of the eternal beatitude. But we find also in the most authentic Christianity an apophatic approach to the Godhead, a *via negationis*, through which the soul proceeds mostly by rejection and negation. God is unlike everything else, and he who wants to contemplate him as he is in himself must transcend not only the plane of imagery, but also the plane of concept—our last and most dangerous idols.

This way of negation is not without a biblical basis: the Old Testament calls God the Hidden One: *Tu es Deus absconditus*, and no image of him was ever allowed. The New Testament insists even more on this transcendence of God. Saint Paul describes the knowledge of him through faith as a reflection in a mirror and as an enigma: *videmus per speculum in aenigmate*, and Saint John affirms *Deum nemo vidit unquam* (nobody has ever seen God). Apophatism was more and more emphasized by the Greek Fathers: Saints Basil, Gregory Nazianzen, Gregory of Nyssa, and Saint John Chrysostom. In the polemic against Arianism and chiefly against Eunomius, Saint Gregory of Nyssa extols the incomprehensibility, the unintelligibility of God, whom neither speech nor thought can ever attain. His hymn to the unknown God (recently translated into Sanskrit) sounds like an advaitic hymn—a fully Christianized advaitic one. Evagrius (at the end of the fourth century) follows the same apophatic paths; he rejects even supernatural visions in order to adhere to the Godhead in its absolute purity. He refers to the infinite nescience in which the mystic is immersed.

Dionysius, the Pseudo-Areopagite (an unknown Syrian at the end of the fifth or the beginning of the sixth century) gave theological shape to the apophatism of the Greek Fathers. He distinguishes three levels of theology: the positive, the negative, and the supereminent. Positive theology asserts the propositions: God is just, good, etc.... Negative theology denies to God those qualities, because he is not just, good, etc... in the same way as creatures are. He is infinitely beyond them all. This negative degree has a purifying role. The third degree, called supereminent, asserts once again what the previous degree has denied, but not in the same way. Does the third degree recapture the first degree with an infinite exponent, as most of the medieval doctors, chiefly Saint Thomas Aquinas, interpreted the Dionysian ascent? It seems, rather, that this supereminent theology is, above all, a deeper immersion into the abyss of nescience; the more the mystic contemplates God and experiences him—*patiens divina*—the more does he measure an unplumbed depth of the 'supra-divine Deity'. Scotus Erigena (ninth century) was a faithful exponent of Dionysism.

The Flemish and the German Schools of mysticism were deeply marked by medieval Areopagitism. Hadewijch in her poems on divine love is but a prelude to the highest contemplation found in Meister Eckhart and Ruysbroeck. Eckhart sharply distinguishes God from the Godhead. The divine Being is called God inasmuch as he is related. In its absoluteness it must be called only Godhead: the unspeakable, the unthinkable One. The orthodoxy of some of

Eckhart's paradoxal utterances was challenged, and Pope John XXII condemned twenty-six of his propositions, but his disciples Tauler and Suso are undoubtedly entirely orthodox. So also was the greatest of the Flemish mystics, Ruysbroeck and in the fifteenth century the great German thinker Cardinal Nicholas of Cusa. What is striking in Ruysbroeck's mysticism is the perfect synthesis of extreme apophatism with the deepest trinitarian vision. At the ultimate point of the experience, of the union without difference, there still remains the distinction between the essence of God and the essence of soul, founded as it is upon the very distinction of the divine Persons from one another. The same fusion of trinitarian contemplation with the contemplation of the oneness of the Deity is conspicuous in Saint John of the Cross. Only once does he use the term *Deidad* (Deity). In the *Living Flame of Love* he describes the awakening of God within the innermost recesses of the soul; then the soul knows God with the very knowledge by which God knows himself and loves him with the very love with which he loves himself. At this apex of the mystical rebirth the Holy Spirit creates in that soul an aspiration entirely ineffable. Therefore, just as in Ruysbroeck, the distinctiveness of the divine Persons is perceived at the very moment of the vision of their Oneness—beyond it, or rather within it.

Christian mysticism is then, in its essence, the sharing of God's life; that is, the sharing of the trinitarian relationship. It is an intuition above image and concept, a direct experience—not a man-made one, but a God-given one—existential contact with what God is in himself and for himself.

Therefore we are facing two main problems when we try to compare by analogies and contrasts Christian mysticism with Hindu mysticism. Is the Vedantic vision of Being, *sat*, a challenge to our traditional post-aristotelian ontology? Are we invited to reshape the very basis of our ontology? In a parallel way, is not the mystical experience of the triune divine Being an appeal to reconsider our idea of *esse*? The divine existence is a personal one, but not a mono-personal one. God is not *it*, is not *he*, is not *I*, but rather he is *I* and *I* and *I*. His very essence is identical with tri-personal relationship. Therefore, is not every *esse* a *co-esse*, every *sat* a *samsat*, every *being* a *being-together?*

Perhaps the notion of person also has to be reshaped. Since the person in God is relationship itself, an *esse ad alterum*, a being for and towards the other as other (and the otherness of each divine Person from the Others is necessarily infinite), it seems that the essence of personality lies in relationship towards other persons and mainly towards the divine Persons, an *esse ad alterum, esse ad Te, homo*, and ultimately an *esse ad Te, Christe, ad Te, Spiritus, ad Te, Pater*. The dialogue between Hindu mysticism and Christian mysticism must be located at this metaphysical and theological level: nothing short of that dialogue can break the wall. Christian mysticism is trinitarian or it is nothing. Hindu thought, so deeply focused on the Oneness of the One, on the *kevalin* in his *kevalatva*, cannot be sublimated into trinitarian thought without a crucifying dark night of the soul. It has to undergo a noetic metamorphosis, a passion of the spirit.

Meanwhile, our task is to keep all doors open, to wait with patience and theological hope for the hour of the advent of India into the Church, in order to realize the fullness of the Church and the fullness of India. In this age-long vigil, let us remember that very often *amor intrat ubi intellectus stat ad ostium* (Love can enter where the intellect must stand at the door).

Monchanin's thought, naturally given to make the imaginative and speculative leap from paradox to recon-ciliation, can be called trinitarian. He transforms platonic ideas into transubstantiated reality by Christ, both in the now and the parousia. Not only is his thought trinitarian but each meditation and his style itself can be called trinitarian: polarities are identified and transubstantiated. His style like his thought moves in concentric waves, and both seem to be structured like a series of harmonious and deepening medi-tations. This again makes one think of Pascal. The light of certitude that one finds in Monchanin is not lumen *but* fulgur, *not a gradual illumination but a fulguration, the fire of certitude. It is the explosion of truth in a great speculative mind and an immense imagination.*

TIME AND THE ETERNAL [8]

THE PHILOSOPHICAL PROBLEM of the relationship between time and the Eternal is found in Greece (the eternity of the intelligible world, the temporality of the sensible world); in India (the eternity of *Brahman-Atman*, the temporality of *Triloka* and *Pudgala*; in China the eternity of *Tao*), the temporality of phenomena subject to the modalities of *yin* and *yang*; and among modern thinkers (Descartes, cf. Jean Wahl, *Du rôle de l'idée de l'instant dans la philosophie de Descartes*; Spinoza, moving from the fourth to the fifth part of the Ethics; Kant, the eternity of noumenon and the temporality of phenomenon; Hegel, hypostatized becoming...; in the eighteenth and nineteenth centuries, scientific expansion of time; Bergson, the state of becoming identified with duration, and eternity with the fullness of duration; Heidegger, the finitude of time and of Being; for a theory of generalized relativity, universe=space-time).

The religious problem, little in evidence among the Greeks and outside religions of revelation (where time is minimized religiously, the essential is non-historical) is, on the contrary, crucial in religions based on revelation, such as Judaism, Christianity, Islam; above all in Christianity, which is a religion of salvation through the Incarnation, an event in history; in Judaism, creation in time, revelation by stages:

Abraham, Moses, the eschatological Messiah; in Islam: cf.
Islamic temporalization.

Some examples. Saint Paul's vocabulary: *aion, plenitudo
temporis* (the fullness of time); the first and last Adam; the
increase of Christ *in mensuram plenitudinis aetatis Christi;*
eschatology. Origen: Platonism rectified by the event of the
Savior's Epiphany. Augustine: the same—cf. *Confessions* I,
13; realism of time; the maturation and the building of the
City of God (cf. Guitton, *Time and Eternity according to
Plotinus and Saint Augustine*).[9]   Boethius, *Consolation of
Philosophy:* 'Time the moving image of eternity.'   The
Middle Ages lived on Augustine and Aristotle. The acute
sense of time for modern man—Kierkegaard: kierkegaardian
'repetition' as opposed to Nietzchean 'eternal return.'
Newman and the idea of ecclesial and dogmatic development.

It is difficult, if not impossible, to unite the two terms
time and eternity in a single purely philosophical synthesis.
Either time is denied (acosmism: Śankara) or detemporalized
(cyclic-time: Pythagorean) or reduced to a pure function of
sign (Plato: the eternal is *to ontos on*, the temporal *oxia
ontos*); or the Eternal is negated (positivism) or reduced to a
mirage (pragmatism) or elaborated non-philosophically (Bergson) or finally thrust back into the impenetrability of mystery.
The congenital (consubstantial?) tendency in philosophy to
reduce one of the two terms to the epiphenomenon of the
other. The temporal is identified with the sensible and the
eternal with the intelligible; their relation becomes that of
sign to the thing signified, of evidence to truth. And while
the eternal desingularizes and depersonalizes itself—to the
limit, the place of abstract relations—the temporal loses all
contact with it other than notional contact and is dissipated in
a becoming without fullness.

Religious thought, especially Christian religious thought,
affirms with equal emphasis time, the eternal, and their constant coordination. Through the eternal which is infused
(immanent) in it, the temporal acquires an absolute
coefficient. Perhaps the relation of time to the eternal is
thinkable only from the perspective of the time of the

deification of creation, and of the eternity of the deifying Trinity, by assuming in its circumincession the totality of the world.

Time of deification (*theosis*). All chronology is a 'logo-chronia' (a metaphysics of time requires the temporalizations of the Word). No time, apart from this unique and total becoming of the Word causes becoming.

Analysis discerns as many zones of becoming as ontological zones: the zone of the universe, more exactly cosmic time; the zone of life, of each living thing, of the totality of living things (the biosphere); the zone of the spirit, of each consciousness and the duration of the totality of consciousness (dialectic, noosphere). The becoming of the biosphere, incommensurable with cosmic time is, however, coordinated to it; the becoming of the noosphere, coordinated to that of the biosphere is, however, commensurable with it.

A third becoming is incarnated in the other two and links them to the eternal: the Christic becoming. The time of the Christosphere or of the Mystical Body belongs simultaneously and entirely to a double economy. In so far as it is visible, the *body* of the Word Incarnate, it belongs to the economy of the becoming of the Church, of the Spirit, of life, of the world. In so far as it is invisible, the body of the *Word*, it belongs to the economy of the eternal circumincession 'which expands unity into Trinity and gathers Trinity into unity'. The Incarnation saturates time with the eternal (the Johannine *kai nun*) and confers on becoming ontologized by Christ the absolute gift of the eternal.

THE PLURALITY OF TIME

1. COSMIC TIME

I N THE UNIVERSE: no immobility, no stopping: *panta
rei.* Substantialization of movement. (Bergson: *Creative
Evolution, Thought and Movement*; Le Roy: *La Pensée
intuitive, L'Exigence idéaliste et le fait de l'évolution.*[10]
Time: flux itself, the rhythm of flux; rhythm: periods of
tension and periods of release.

Newton turned both time and space into absolutes, coordinated receptacles: the postulate of isochronia (homo-
genious time). The theory of generalized relativity broke this
newtonian figuration. Einstein (after Minkowsky) constructed
a quadrimensional continuum: the three dimensions of space
(Riemannian) and that assumed by the imaginary index $\sqrt{-1}$,
time. This space-time is not the receptacle of matter-energy
but is identical to it, space expressing the simultaneity of
events of the universe ($=$ a phenomenon located in space-
time) and time, their expansion (De Sitter, Lemaître).

The becoming of the universe is the history of space-time.
We study its origin, its end, or its rhythm (indefinite
expansion leading to dispersion, or a period alternating
expansion and retraction?) and the number of this rhythm.
We can merely note periodic returns, constants. Is not
homogeneity of the time of the universe itself still a
postulate? Is the temporal scale the same in microphysics as

137

in macrophysics?

From the perspective of the expanding universe, there is properly speaking no return. No element of the universe is at the same point twice—and time represents the axis of expansion. Likewise there is no corpuscular individuality in microphysics outside of configuration, likewise there is no configuration outside the tension of the totality of the extending and expanding universe. (In the inorganic world itself, a time which is somehow analogous to that of living things takes shape: that of chemical species in the process of disintegration—radium—or of integration.)

2. BIOLOGICAL TIME

The time of living things is irreducible to cosmic time; it is non-homogenious, qualitative, and continuous.

1) The *elements of living things* possess a relative automony in relation to the living itself; an incomplete synthesis, whence the possibility of sickness (the meta-physical foundation of sickness: the biological multiple rebels against unification). Thus the dream of *yoga*, of Taoism— borrowed to some extent by modern naturist medicine and homeopathy—of reuniting elements which escape, either making consciousness enter into the very organism (*yoga*, Taoism) or regenerating them by passivity in regard to nature. Lapicque has shown that a local time exists for innervated muscles. Chronaxia. The autonomy of living things relative to the time of life.

2. *Living things*. The local time of muscles, organs (time of arteries, heart, crystallin, perhaps of cells and elements of cells) are relatively coordinated by the particular time of living things, in a healthy unifying organism. (The *one* of the time of the living in the multiple of its elements.) The experiments of Voronoff and Dartigue would tend to show the important role of sexual time: the rejuvenation of the whole organism by a testicular graft. Lecomte du Noüy has shown by the cicatrization index the heterogenious and qualitative character of time in man, time which is in the process of

slowing down from childhood to old age. (See also Minkowsky, *Le Temps vécu* and Mourgue and Monakoff, *Introduction biologique à l'étude de la psychologie*.)

3) *Species*. Although the species cannot be assimilated by a survivor, it seems to constitute a biological unit of a superior kind; it has birth (genesis), growth, and decline.

4) *Biosphere*. No species is isolatable from all others and from planetary epochs: the term biosphere connotes this universal interrelation and this geological dependence.

Transformism, the only form by which we can understand the succession of species, seems itself to be hardly explicable, unimaginable developments of mutations, that is, if we do not turn to the hypothesis of an ultimate biological unit, the biosphere. One season and only one for the appearance of life, by spontaneous generation; one season and only one for the advent, development, stagnation or death of four or five great biological layers from the paleozoic era to man. The mode of passing from one species to another remains very obscure, even if the passing seems undeniable. Individual mutations in the course of embryonic life seem however insufficient. They must have been amplified by a kind of common resonator and they must themselves be linked to the *global* transformation of a species, probably in connection with the variations of the inhabited layer of the earth (Seuss' use of the term biosphere). Such a genesis took place perhaps on a very large surface (ologenesis). There is a sudden leap from one species to another, a very short *quantum*, genetic continuity, and morphological discontinuity. Each species constitutes a related whole. And one can go from one to the other without a total recasting of the organism, a recasting, occurring of course not accidentally but by broad layers, which reacts in its turn upon the totality of life. The appearance of a new species is compensated by a lowering of potential in the others.

Thus we find, on the biospheric level, a homologue of the elements of living beings, of the living itself, of species. Total biological time is the time of the biosphere. Each of the great biological layers marks the age of this time. It is not cyclical—never a return; nor is it homogeneous—slow periods of orthogenesis follow sudden thrusts of mutations; rhythm of tension and of release, which is essentially qualitative (inventions and quasi-repetitions), quantitative only in connection with space. In so far as they are spatialized, species may be synchronous (simultaneity in space) in their successive pulsions. Cosmic time sustains spatially biospheric time, which is genesis and growth.

3. TIME OF THE SPIRIT

Man arises from life as life arises from matter. He inserts his own duration into the time of the biosphere, just as the latter is bound to the time of the universe. This duration is far more analogous to the becoming of life than to that of the world. Like it and more than it, it is a heterogeneous qualitative continuity.

1) *Time of Consciousness.* Strictly speaking, it is duration such as Bergson analyzed it, irreducible to juxtaposition *partes extra partes*; continuity of presence, which is revealed to us by memory and by which the present, far from being fixed at one point, appears to us affected by volumosity capable of indefinite extension both retrospectively and prospectively. The past is wholly past and the future wholly future only by their dependence on the cosmos. In so far as they are purely conscious, their distance disappears. However continuous the duration may be—of conscious and subconscious, both permeable—it is not, however, at all uniform. It has its sluggish periods, its sudden stops, surges, breaks, involutions. A rhythm without law, which creates itself by the predominance of certain themes (individuality, the very structure of such singular themes).

Duration is equivalent to creation and freedom. It is the unforeseeable maturation of oneself. The self is never given to itself. It does not possess itself but it seeks itself. It is its own search, a search which has no end except in the Endless. The presence of the self to the self is also Parousia. Duration in itself has nothing in common with space. It is pure temporality. Between two durations, there cannot be simultaneity but rather presence. —But there is no pure duration. In a living being all duration is given in organic connection with space, and through space simultaneity becomes possible. Synchronism = syntropism. For duration, growth is thus not a simple extension or prolongation, but rather interiorization. Creating oneself means giving shape to one's interior life, spiritualizing oneself. Consciousness should be represented not by an infinitely receding line, but by a spiral which coils around itself, the image of increasing interiorization, of density. States of tension are states of at least possible intuition, of creation, of freedom. States of release correspond intellectually to the level of speech, actively to the level of habit, and affectively to the level of emotion.

Duration and Creation. Duration being identified with creation, the problem of the relation between creation and construction arises as a function of temporality. Is this not the relation between rhythm and structure (musicality and architecture) between *pneuma* and *logos*? If we say that creation is time itself, then construction is intelligible spatially, the support and indispensable mediation for creation. In order not to disappear, creation must be reimmersed in construction in order to burst forth again in an unending circumincession.

Duration and Affinity. The problem of the coexistence of consciousness is a problem not of simultaneity, nor of inter-actions, but of a call, a presence, and a gift. Three degrees, corresponding to three modes of knowledge: by mimicry, by intellectual intuition, by love.

Knowledge by means of mimetic imitation (an actor's) is brought about through the most external signs, without allowing us to discern whether they rightly or wrongly convey the true personality. It refers the other to the self: hence its extrinsicism.

The Bergsonian type of intuition, or the effort of *temporary* coincidence with another consciousness, refers the self and the other to a third term; for example, to a type (through a given artist one tries to reach a psychology of art). At best one reaches being only such as it is, not as it will be, or might be: scientific disinterestedness, neither fusion nor call.

Knowledge of the third kind is that of unqualified love, referring the I to the other as other, through decentration, *extasis*. It alone reaches the other in the center of interiority and in the vital impulse. In itself it is creative, both for the other and for itself (cf. note on the ecstatic, oscillating, eschatological nature of love).

Duration and Values. Freedom, which is duration, is not merely being unattached or merely going beyond. It is centered by values and polarized by intentionality toward the other self, toward the 'thou' (cf. axiology).

2) *Time of the Noosphere*. The coming of man signifies a radical change of perspective. Before him life was a means for the species and the species for the biosphere. No longer can man be considered as a means; he constitutes in his order a definitive end. The human world is pluralistic and monadic. How can we go from monadism to monadology? How can we find unity in becoming through convergence? Is not this creation of unity which leaves to each consciousness its own finality the work of supra-consciousness? Through the subconscious, man vitally communicates with other men as with nature; through consciousness he selects certain others through whom he foresees all (*agapè* anticipated by love); through supra-consciousness or axiological consciousness, man vitally communicates with others in values: action, art, science.

We can see the noosphere as the dependence of the totality of these values in relation to the biosphere and especially in relation to humanity as a biological species—their static interdependence on the level of universalism—and finally their temporal growth which has its own rhythm. The noosphere is born with man and remains until *homo sapiens* almost imperceptible. It asserts itself with him; it knows periods of inventive mutations and orthogenesis. It is dispersed and is reconstituted. ('We civilizations know we are mortal'—Valéry.) It evolves along a spiral rather than a vertical line and slowly it acquires the sense of the universal—modern technology being a homologue of the nervous system—and it advances toward an end which is impenetrable. Is it supra-humanity or assumption into another sphere which would be to it what it is to the biosphere?

To the extent that humanism tends toward panhumanism, it perceives its finiteness, the transitoriness of every form, of every canon. In this way it anticipates relatively closed civilizations: Hellenism, India, China, etc., a spiritual reality of which they would be the unsubordinated component, a reality of finality by means of which individual consciousness is integrated into a given civilization. In the same way, any growth of lucidity increases yearning. Humanism goes beyond humanism.

The scale of time of the noosphere, without analogy to the scale of time of individuals, develops in broad layers. A thousand years are like a lifetime (think of the duration of languages or of types of civilization).

Biological analogies which are so often used are imprecise and often false. The duration of the noosphere must be compared, not to vital time, but to duration. Rather, in the same way as for man, there is a connection between duration and spatialized time. As *creation*, values have rhythm in duration, and as sociological objects, they are enunciated in time.

If duration is the fabric of the noosphere, as it is for each consciousness, there must be a dialectics of human history. Many lives are illuminated only at death. Perhaps only eschatology will provide the key to human tragedy. Reconstituting it means through extrapolation, forming a curve of which we can only recognize a short segment. Every philosophy of history involves a similar hypothesis. In this dialectic which, for us, is unforeseeable, civilizations are moments that are irreplaceable but totally surpassable. No cycles. *Growth*, not in the mode of plants but in the noetic mode, under the guiding image of a symphony in which

civilizations would be the interrelated themes. Hegel reconstituted this dialectic of the spirit such as it appeared to him:
his viewpoint arbitrary, even disappointing (the Prussian
state!) and the application of the ternary rhythm somewhat
mechanical. The rhythm of the dialectics of the noosphere is
not necessarily uniform. It is, quite the contrary, polymor-
phous.

4. THE BECOMING OF THE CHRISTOSPHERE

The christosphere, the end of the noosphere, as the latter
is of the biosphere and as the biosphere is of the cosmos, is
its own finality. It takes upon itself all being and hence all
becoming of everything below it. And it is not without
radical change: cosmic time is the time of expansion, vital
time that of organization, human time that of creation. The
time of the Church is that of reception because it is the
intemporal rhythm of God, the Trinitarian circumincession
received in the becoming, which has become the Christic and
pneumatic rhythm of deification. Being coextensive with the
becoming of man, of life and of the world, this Christic
becoming is, from the creation (perhaps *ab aeterno*) to the
baptism of Jesus, the time of the gestation of Christ borne by
the world; from the messianic consecration to the Passion, the
time of the Epiphany; from the Resurrection (death of Jesus,
Easter, Pentecost) to the Parousia, the time of the Incorporation of Christ bearing the world. This radical change
from creation to reception, passing from the becoming of the
noosphere to that of the christosphere, is the temptation of
man—mortal to humanity and vivification. The time of Christ
is one, as Christ is one. Through him and in him, the eternal
is received into the temporal. The time of the noosphere, of
the biosphere, of the cosmos is eternalized. Eternity is
temporalized. This becoming—this extensional tension which
is interiorized from the cosmos to man through life, and in
fullness in Christ and eternity—and this pure tension of
expansion which is circumincession are unified in the Pleroma.

5. TIME AND THE ETERNAL

Cosmic time is expansion, if not spatial (Lemaitre's hypothesis) [then] at least according to becoming, a becoming which is not haphazard but ordered, numbered, rhythmic— that is to say, periodic groups whose totality is perhaps not periodic but expansive, certainly not periodic if we consider, as we must, the universe not in isolation but in its ordination to life. Cosmic time subtends and conditions biological time. Biological time, in all its modalities, elements, individuals, species, biosphere, is rhythm of a different kind from cosmic time: periodicities incomparably less marked (and only by spatial connections), definite, visible expansion. Unmeasured number, unforeseeableness, newness; alternation between tension and relative release: tension being especially marked at the advent of each species, and in certain phases of each individual; release especially marked in periods of ortho-genesis.

This vital time appears only through the mediation of a structure which conditions it and limits it: organism, form. Biological time is the becoming of organization. In living things form is matter (no other element than in non-living things) and duration, the rhythm of organization which is life.

The becoming of man: duration inserts itself into vital time and through it into cosmic time, due to the life of the organism. In itself, duration is rhythm, still more interiorized in relation to the rhythm of matter: rhythm which grasps itself through consciousness (identity in the moment of *cogito*, between temporalizing time and temporalized time) and self engenders self. Freedom is this genesis. The becoming of man can be called equivalently time of consciousness, time of freedom, time of creation. Values, the axis of this interior rhythm, would be the spiritual transposition of the mathematical norm of the cosmos, of the organizing idea of life.

Between intuition and speech there is a relationship analogous to the one between rhythm and structure. Speech conditions and limits intuition. In man, the soul is nothing other than the rhythm of the axiological freedom of creation. Human duration is creative time. The maxima of consciousness, freedom, invention—of tension—coincide. Such maxima are conditioned phenomenally (but subordinated metaphysically) to the minima of psychophysiological phenomenonology, of determinism, of speech—of release. All becoming, extensional tension, signifies a gap between being and being, a possibility and an impossibility of rejoining: maximum gap in cosmic time and minimum in duration. A unification of the multiple which grows by degrees, matter not being particularly unified by time, life being more so in the unity of form, and consciousness much more so in a unity which is for the first time interior. The essence of the finite, of the non-absolute, is to possess oneself only partially, for the finite is movement, movement of expansion, organization, intentionality. Consciousness is by its nature ecstatic. The gap between *extasis* and *enstasis* creates time. Privileged moments realize this conjunction of *extasis* and *enstasis* in a partial and precarious, but still real, way, yet still only figuratively and dynamically. And this is the eternal in the moment, the *sign* of the unqualified eternal.

The eternal is not set in opposition to time as its antithesis or its correlative (as space is the correlative of time) but as its limit, its absolute: tension without release, rhythm without structure, unconditioned activity. The Absolute is unqualified freedom. Circumincession, supra-temporal rhythm of the triune unity of the Triad One; tension of being, of thought, of love, absolute One-multiple; unity of *extasis*, of the Father in the Word and the Spirit, of the Word in the Spirit and the Father, of the Spirit in the Word and the Father, and of *enstasis* circumincession. All becoming mimes, represents, imitates this rhythm of ecstatic *enstasis* and of enstatic *extasis*. Cosmic time mimes it in the spatial, life represents it through forms, man imitates it through his enstatic consciousness and his ecstatic love, deified man brings it into reality in finite modes by participating substantially in the Trinitarian rhythm; Christ bringing it into reality in fullness unifies in his Pleroma the supratemporal rhythm of the Absolute and the temporal rhythm of the created.

CREATION

PSEUDO-DIONYSIUS attempts to make creation intelligible, in so far as a mystery can be intelligible, by the diffusive essence of Being: *ens diffusivum sui.* This same axiom could be applied to transcendentals. The *one* is the generator of the multiple by setting itself up, setting itself in opposition to the other than the one, to the other one, uniting itself with this other one.... This diffusivity, which is a necessary consequence in a metaphysics which identifies being and substance, becomes the very definition of being in an ontololgy which identifies (as does Bergsonism) being with ordination, *esse* with *esse ad.* In a metaphysics of communion, where *co-esse* is first in relation to *esse*, being is not only diffusive, but is *diffusivity.* Being is, only through its relationship of communion: *Esse* is interior to *co-esse.*

But true being is person: true communion is communion of persons. Person is 'diffusive' of itself through love; and it is at least radical love which constitutes person in so far as it is person (*esse ad alium*). The *co-esse* of persons is communion according to love, and it is within this *co-esse* that the person is person. (The metaphysics of *esse ad.* The substantialization of movement and the metaphysics of communion are identified with each other in the metaphysics of person (*esse ad, esse tecum*, tension of communion.) In the absolute, movement and communion are identical: tension of intra-trinitary communion according to the eternal, circumincession. In the relative, they are distinct: tension of communion according to the temporal. This non-coincidence of tension and of communion characterizes creation, constitutes the relative, generates eternalized becoming (glory), incarnates the Word, modalizes the Incarnation (Redemption), distinguishes the Church even in glory (capacity for creation, Incarnation, Redemption, Church, Pleroma, because it is the capacity of non-absolute, absolutizable persons).

The Trinity is the mystery of the Godhead elucidating itself to itself in Alterity, completing itself and returning in the other Alterity of unitive Love.

There is a divine auto-genesis, a becoming of God, but an eternal becoming,[11] pure tension without extension. Tension of communion, unity of *co-esse*. Each Person is constitutive of this unity through that which constitutes him as person: his ordination to the two Others. The internal theophany of God (circumincession) is comprised of three terms: Mystery, Logos, Love. Logos is the Epiphany of Mystery to itself; Love, the unity of Mystery and its Epiphany.

Each Person of the Trinity is ordained absolutely to the other two and relatively to creation which is deified by the incarnation of the Word and the mission of the Spirit. The Father is ordained to the Word and to the Spirit in the Trinity and (according to a relative ordination absolutizing itself to the Word incorporating the world) to the Spirit completing the Pleroma. In the same way, the Word is ordained absolutely to the Father and to the Spirit and relatively to the Paracleto-Pleroma and to the Father, the source and end of deification. The Spirit, ordained absolutely to the Word and to the Father is ordained relatively to the Mystical Body and to the Father, the alpha and omega of creation. This is because each Trinitarian Person, as Person, is absolute diffusivity towards the other two, and relative diffusivity, that is freely and superabundantly, in regard to finite, angelic, or human persons. The very infinity of his diffusibility opens up the possible without assignable limit. The trinitarian *co-esse*, in so far as it is perfect inclusion, opens up the possible without limit: inclusion through superabundance, of finite persons, angels, and men. The Trinity, the *co-esse* of the three Persons, is thus perfect inclusion of perfect diffusivities.

Creation has no being except through its relationship—intemporal with God, [12] intemporal with created things, [13] of absolute dependence with regard to the Trinity. Its being is totally sign, Epiphany of God. What is epiphany for the world is kenosis for God. By reflecting itself through superabundance of personality and of circumincession in its images, the Trinity attenuates in some way both its Persons and its Unity.

The universe and above all man have a trinitarian configuration—of mystery, of epiphany, of unitive love—but where neither unity nor plurality ever fully appear. They seem even to be opposed. *Co-esse* is only approximated, and the temptation remains to seek it in identity more than in communion. The universe is the multiple kenosis of God, but a kenosis which conditions epiphany and which calls forth an inverse kenosis of creation, which, no longer waiting to appear to itself, wishes only to be a sign of the Trinity. It is a sign which becomes substantial in so far as it is pure sign.

Are not his kenosis and this epiphany to be identified with the absolute ordination of the world to God, that is, with deification?

Being subordinated to God signifies receiving everything (ontological passivity). Now, what is received is the movement received, and there is no movement outside of ordination to the essential movement of deification.

Ontological passivity becomes and even is the capacity for deification. Creation is thus identified with deification, with the Mystical Body. Deification, the union with God, is accomplished through Christ who is one with God. The participation of man with God through Christ and the unity of Christ with God are reciprocal functions originating in God; that is, man is deified to the extent that Christ integrates himself as the person personalizing his personalized

person.[14]   Christ's *co-esse* with God is total from the
beginning. With man it is progressive. The eternal distinction between Christ and those 'Christified' derives from
the fact that for the humanity of Christ deification is acquired
from the time of the Incarnation; whereas for the 'Christified'
deification is, in time, a limit inaccessible although present
through its assimilative and increasing attraction, and in the
eternal, a reality participated in, an assimilation, perhaps still
increasing, in the divinity of Christ.

The Word was made becoming: that is, time (terrestrial
life of Jesus, duration, the interior of Jesus) and dialectical
becoming (Christ glorious and the Mystical Body). Identifying
himself with becoming, he thus assumes in a certain way the
evil coextensive with becoming (*factus peccatum*: essential
kenosis), he identifies becoming with self (deifying Redemption and joy correlative and coextensive with suffering),
according to a becoming, never closed, even absolutized. This
becoming is essentially that of man and that of the world (the
place of life). Christ can be said to personalize persons,
vitalize life, ontologize the world.

Thus Christ is *primogenitus*. In him all things have
solidity. He is the first created, the only one created: unique
Person, uniquely Person, indissolubly humain, cosmic, and
Trinitarian. In him creation goes from God to God through
God.

Creation is actually intelligible only between the redemptive Incarnation (Pentecost) and the Parousia. It is the
reciprocal love of the Trinity and the Pleroma:[15]   Being,
Knowledge, and Love and the *Co-esse* of the Three in the
Trinity and in the Pleroma, which are united in the double
and the unique *co-esse* of Christ, in his Church.

The Church is the Absolute made into mystical body. It is
the *totum esse ad hominem, totum ad Deum* in fullness; the
total Christ present *et nunc* in his movement (in his essence)
but temporally and spatially past and to come, and
fragmented and delayed in the effectuations of his movement,
in his history. This delay is inherent in the very becoming.
Sin which is coextensive with becoming (not as distinct but as

separated from the eternal) intensifies it immensely: there is evil inherent in the *visible* Church, his *corpus peccatum*, his Passion which lasts for all time even in the Eucharist. But it is evil redeemed, a Passion announcing the Resurrection. The Church, identical with Christ in his Spirit, is distinct from Christ in his history—but Christ's history is not separable even in glory from his essence. Christ, identical with God in the eternal mode, remains distinct in the historical mode, even in glory: man. In Him alone history and essence coincide. In the Church essence is the limit of history.

Creation, the superabundance of the diffusivity of the three Persons and of their *co-esse*—unlimited manifestation of the possible called forth to being, to Trinitarian inclusion—is simultaneously kenosis and epiphany of God. God veils his Unity, he veils his Trinity. He creates a world from which life is born, a life from which man rises up, a humanity from which Christ emerges. An ever deepening kenosis: in Christ it appears more moving than in man, than in life, than in the world. An increasing Epiphany: with the advent of thought God is known, loved; with the advent of Christ he is revealed and participated in. The glory of God is Epiphany through kenosis: an external theophany which flows forth from the superabundance of the internal theophany, the manifestation of the One in Three and the drawing of the Three into One. It culminates in the Passion-Resurrection, in which the very human figuration which Christ took on in order to empty himself disappears, and from which the resurrected Christ comes forth. It remains in the Church, the body of sin and body of Christ; in the Eucharist, where nothing other than pure sign can be grasped. In it is brought about the conversion of the world, of life, of man. The world is only for life, and life for man, and man is not for himself. All is sign, but a true and substantial sign of the One who through love of creation made himself into sign.

PANCHRISTISM

ALL THINGS have solidity in him: *In ipso*, matter (cf. *Philosophy of Matter*), life (the biosphere finalized by the noosphere, itself finalized by the christosphere), humanity (one in the Second Adam), the Church (which is his Body). Through him, *per ipsum*, all things are brought back in the Spirit to the Father. In the end, Christ will be *omnia in omnibus* (*pan en pasin*). At the Parousia, literally *everything* will become Christ, without pantheism, without absorption. Just as matter is not absorbed but integrated in living things, without the addition of new elements or compounding, just as life is not absorbed but integrated through thought without addition or compounding (there is no true dualism in man), so those Christified will not be absorbed but integrated in Christ who establishes their personality through this very integration.

PANCHRISTISM AND PANTHEISM

According to the idea of Father Auguste Valensin,[16] pantheism, always a temptation for philosophy, would basically be a sort of metaphysical equivalent of a theology of the Incarnation extended to all being, a hypostatic union of God with each creature.

What makes such a view disappointing is that it goes

beyond the possibilities of philosophical speculation and it lacks a unique center, a personality personalizing all persons.

From the point of view of both the philosophy of the person and panchristism, the hypostatic union of the Word with all consciousness is a reality, but not through the equivalence of consciousness either among themselves or with God. The transcendence of the Totally-Other is maintained; the differentiation of souls is established absolutely by their insertion in the Absolute; for them to be, their subordination in relation to Christ is not only postulated but required.

Thus without a pantheistic leveling off, *God-intoxication*, which is the mysticism of pantheism, is completing itself in the universal Christ. *Panchristism = Christocentric pantheism.* Every creature is hypostatically united to the Word to the extent (always imperfect, always finite but always real) that it is united to Christ. Absolute panchristism is a limit-state, even in glory. But if it is movement which is hypostatized, the movement toward Christ, who is All in all, is substantially Christified.

PANCHRISTISM AND THE TRINITY

Total Christian mysticism is a Christic mysticism which ends in Trinitarian mysticism in unity. There is no access to the one and triune God outside the mediation of him who is Mediator between the Trinity and Creation, because in the order of eternal processions he is already Mediator between the Father and the Spirit.

The ritual and spiritual participation in the mystery of the dead and risen Christ ends in the Pleroma, where the very mystery of Christ raising the world with him ends. The highest panchristic personalization establishes, as it metamorphoses them, the knowledge and love of man for God in the knowledge and love of the Man-God for God. This means that in glory the elect know the Three Persons not with knowledge through an intellectual intermediary (knowledge through a mirror, *per speculum*, like faith) nor through immediate solitary knowledge, but through the *mediation* of the knowledge of the Word incarnate—a mediation which, however, does not introduce a duality. It becomes ours. Filled with his knowledge, the elect are also filled with his love. They love the Father through the love of the Word who is the Spirit.

Thus Trinitarian insertion far from being beyond Christ is the embrace of Christ. By meeting him in his essential movement toward the Spirit and toward the Father, man, once fully Christified, substantially shares, without intermediary, without the separateness of personality (for his personality consists in the diminishing of all separateness), in the divine circumincession. As human knowledge becomes Christic knowledge, as human love becomes pneumatic, they come to their proper end, their proper desire, their proper essence. A coming never fixed, a terminus which can only be reached through annihilation. Thus the necessity in glory of an indefinite growth, of a Parousia, of a duration irreductible to time because it is not spatial, filled through and through with eternity, yet ever distinct from the eternity of God who is the only absolute tension.

The finite movements toward God, which persons are, share to an ever-increasing extent (which is their beatitude and being) in the infinite movement of God, which the Trinity is, in this at once finite and infinite movement of God toward God, of God toward the world, and of the world toward God, which the Man-God is.

THE SCHOLASTIC PROBLEM

Medieval thought is divided on the question of the essence of beatitude: for Saint Thomas, knowledge of God; for Saint Bonaventure, love of God. Perhaps this is a false problem.[17] Human faculties do not seem to constitute anything else than the modes and aspects of a fundamental, unifying activity. And if man is in glory, it is the substance of his being which is filled with God without separation. And it is just as impossible to set a noetic source of beatitude in opposition to an affective one as it is to set the Word in opposition to the Paraclete.

THE KINGDOM OF GOD

PASSION AND DEATH

HIS PASSION AND DEATH do not constitute a dramatic change in the career of Jesus. They are the logical outcome (logic of the passion) of the more and more noticeable divergence between the Messianism of Jesus and that of almost all his contemporaries and especially of constituted authorities. The exclusively religious character of Jesus' thought (absence of compromises). Consequences foreseen and accepted by Jesus, not without inner struggles (Gethsemane is the last and culmination of these struggles), through his spirit of submission to the Father.

The coming of the Kingdom of God will be conditioned by moral and physical torture, by the aging and death of the Son of Man. Jesus does not sacrifice merely the hope of his people, including the apostles and his family, but he also sacrifices his popularity, his influence on the crowds, his enthusiasm of the Galilean period. He accepts all—in the night: 'Not what I will but what You will' (Mark 14:36).

Humanly the aftermath of his death will cast even his closest friends into a state of confusion, perhaps of doubt, of despair (Emmaus), and the future of the Kingdom cannot be foreseen and seems irreparably compromised. But still he goes to his death without hesitation.

This renunciation extends to the depths of consciousness. It is the mystery of Gethsemani, where his solidarity with sinful humanity seems to veil the presence of God from him.

That is the great Christian paradox: The Church buried in the tomb. The center of Christianity: *mors et vita* (death and life). 'Unless the seed dies...'. Glorified life, which is a transfiguration, is born from death itself—accepted through love. The last words of Christ: words of abandonment.

RESURRECTION

The new life which Christ receives from the Father is not kept from himself. He appears only to the disciples. Thus no revenge on his enemies. His historical life is something transient, almost unable to be grasped. He seems in a hurry to leave the earthly scene. His apparitions have a far more mystical than empirical character. No numerical increase of believers.

ASCENSION

Cessation of apparitions, signified by a final vision conforming to the given characteristics of the Messiah. Jesus had said: 'It is good for you that I go away.' The personal role passes, so to speak, from the Word to the Spirit. This is the logic of the mediating function of the Word, and this pneumatic life is the Baptism of the Church. Pentecost—with the youthful vigor of the early period. Fecundity: the Christian explosion.

I live, no, it is no longer I....

Saint Paul

PARTICIPATION IN THE TOTAL CHRIST. In terms of analysis this includes an asceticism and a mysticism of Christ and of the Church. These two aspects are in reality one, because it is a question always and only of participating in the Christ of the mystery and in the mystery of Christ.

THE MYSTERY OF DEATH AND LIFE

The infra-mystical level (asceticism). Discontinuity in phenomena and of the degree of intensity, of accent, style, the maximum of activity and the minimum of passivity—and inversely on the mystical level.

ASCETICISM

Infra-mystical spiritual life. Conformity with Christ where personal effort predominates. This conformity with Christ has a negative and a positive aspect.

Negative aspect. Renunciation of evil and mediocrity. Removal of obstacles, i.e. egocentrism in all its forms;

158

unrefined: material goods, greed, sensuality; more refined: self-complacency, stopping with oneself—'Stop, you are so beautiful' (Goethe)—pride (wanting to go beyond by oneself and for oneself): the pride of mystics, the pride of destruction (one's heaven and one's hell).

Positive aspect. Conformity to Christ: virtues (charity) in the form of imitation. Abandonment to God. Adherence to his interior states (seventeenth century French spirituality) which are present in the liturgical cycle and which themselves lead to a simple adherence to the whole of Christ. This adherence is experienced passively: do with me what you will. Absolute openness: the threshold of the mystical life.

Asceticism of the Church. All this renunciation and this conformity to the historical Christ can develop only in the renunciation of oneself to the total Christ and in conformity to him. We must show that the life of the Catholic Christian in the bosom of the Church involves renunciations which are justified for the vitality of the Church and also that his spiritual life is a participation in the collective life of the Church. The opposite of individualistic piety. We must show that the Catholic Christian is associated with the mediating function of Christ in proportion to his spiritual life. Hence he is a co-redeemer (Communion of Saints). 'Each Christian raised up raised up the world' (Elizabeth Leseur). Mediation is a function of the Mystical Body (otherwise the conception of mediation becomes legalistic). This means that there is circulation of a same life within a same body. The asceticism and mysticism of the Church and of the total Christ must be bound to the mystery of God.

THE LITURGY

JUSTIFICATION

HE LITURGY is consistent with the nature of man as an individual and as a social being and with the whole of creation. It conforms to the logic of the Incarnation. It is the prayer of the Christ and the Spirit in the Church. And it carries on the function of the Incarnation.

a. *The nature of man.* We have defined person as the movement of deification which goes from matter to the Trinity through Christ. Man, the mediator between the sense world and the spiritual world, has the function of spiritualizing matter and life. The liturgy is the very sign of this spiritualization, it is the diagram of man.

b. *Society.* There is no society without the communication of values through tangible signs: language, art, etc. Religious values are communicated by this ordered whole of tangible signs which is the liturgy. The spiritual unity of man is reflected in the identity or analogy of formulas and gestures, and the differentiations between natural communities (civilizations) are embodied in the diversity of rites.

c. *Creation.* Saint Paul reveals every creature as groaning and waiting for the Redemption. The priesthood of the living Christ in the Church expressed liturgically accomplishes this Redemption and transforms this groaning into a hymn of praise.

160

d. *The Logic of the Incarnation.* The liturgy follows the logic of the Incarnation. The Word was made flesh, the Infinite finite, the Eternal temporal in order to infuse the Eternal and the Infinite into what is created and to deify man. The liturgy, in the image of the Word, communicates with divine things in tangible form.

e. *The Prayer of Christ in the Church.* Liturgical prayer is not only that of the isolated Christian nor even of all Christian together. It is the prayer of the Church, of Christ himself who is in the Church *semper vivens ad inter-pellandum* and of the Spirit groaning unutterably within it. The essential prayer of the incarnate Christ and the manifested Spirit is modalized into the prayer of the Church and is singularized into the prayer of each of its members. The function of the Incarnation is accomplished through the liturgy as long as time endures.

CYCLES

All civilizations recognize in some way the solar cycle. The Assyro-Babylonians and the Egyptians were the first to calculate exactly the duration of a year: three hundred sixty-five days and a quarter. The Babylonian liturgy probably served as a prototype for that of the Hebrews (the hypothesis of Mowinkel about the feast of the enthronement of Yahweh in Jerusalem imitating the feast of the enthronement of Marduk in Babylon).

The Christian liturgy was structured around the feasts of Easter and Pentecost which prolong and modify the meaning of the Passover and the Jewish Pentecost. (The additional problem of the possible influence of the mystery religions.) In the second century the Epiphany was added (*Ta epiphania*) and in the fourth century Christmas.

The sanctoral and marian cycles came several centuries later (see Delahaye, *Le culte des saints*). The three cycles, christic, marian, and sanctoral, are interwoven. They evoke in the natural unity of one year the multiple unity of the mystery of Christ which human weakness can only encompass singly: it can be grasped through a manifestation in time like the progressive revelation of intuition in speech, projecting the eternalized temporal into the temporal-and-multiple.

The cycle is at the intersection of time and eternity. For example, the time of Advent sets off all human history that preceded Jesus' birth. The time after Pentecost anticipates the whole of the Church's history until the consummation. Other liturgical seasons commemorate both a human phase in the history of Jesus and his glorious history in the Church, still touching on the sensible (Easter and Pentecost), which they condense and represent here and now. No phrase of Christ's Epiphany is in fact merely historical. Each phase subsists in a different—but not less real—mode in the Church. Every liturgical season is a real drama whose truth bears on the past commemorated, on the present (actualization of one aspect of the mystery of Christ in the Church), and on the future prefigured. Evocation, presence, annunciation are the three phases of the temporalization of the Church in which all seasons are eternalized, being gathered into the sacrificial moment.

The three cycles recall within the astronomical unity of one year the interwoven peripli of the total Christ—the first born of all creatures, appearing in the flesh, consuming all things in his Parousia; of his Mother—in a sense coextensive with his; and of his saints—from Adam to the last man. The cycle is the form, and the Mass and the Office its content.

THE EUCHARIST

THE EUCHARIST-SACRAMENT prolongs the Eucharist-sacrifice being referred and subordinated to it.

The Eucharist-sacrifice completes the mediation of Christ, essentially constituted by the Incarnation and culminating in the Passion-Resurrection, giving it its liturgical form, which is sensible, social, figurative, and which realizes the agape.

The presence in the Mystical Body of what is resurrected acquires a fullness compatible with the state of an unresurrected world (what is sensible of the Eucharist species, anticipating the Parousia, becomes true sign and pure sign of presence).

The three essential moments of the Mass (offertory, consecration, communion) are the three moments of Christ's mediation in which the Church is incorporated.

The Offertory—the offering of the species to be transubstantiated—is by that very fact the oblation to the Father in the Spirit of Christ who incorporated humanity in the form of the Church, and thus, in him, in the form of the Church itself and each member.

The Consecration is, through the Spirit, the transubstantiation of the species, realization of the sacramental presence, i.e. the presence in the Mystical Body manifested in the sensible, both figuration and realization of the agape.

It is by that very fact the efficacious call for the trans-figuration of the Church and of each Christian as a member of the Resurrected One.

The Communion completes the rite and the mystery of Christ incarnate offered, dead, resurrected, and communi-cating his Spirit for the glory of the Father. His presence is singularized. For the Church which communicates in each of its members, the absorption of the consecrated species is the efficacious sign of a transformation within him. *Non ego mutabor in te, sed tu mutaberis in me* (I will not be changed in you but you will be changed in me), Christ said to Saint Augustine. A communion of love which initiates in the economy of this world the *co-esse* which will follow the Parousia in the heart of the Trinity.

Mary's motherhood is completed in that of the priesthood, passive like hers and more so than hers (Mary—*prius concepit mente quam corpore;* the priest—*imitamini quod tractatis*, must give birth to God incarnate through his apostolic contemplation before transubstantiating.) Compare the words *concepit de spiritu sancto* and the implicit *epiclesis,* essential to the consecration. The state of Christ in his mortal life exists for his glorious state in the Church, in fullness in the Eucharist.

The Eucharist, the completion of the Incarnation—the body of the Word—is the coming of the Paracletophany. Through the Eucharist the world becomes the pure sign of the Word. It is itself the sign of the agapè, the fullness of charisms through which the Spirit appears. The birth of the Spirit can only be spoken of metaphorically, for he has not taken on a body. But his coming is indeed real, for he has manifested himself, not as the incarnate Word, through tangible signs, but through spiritual signs, the charisms which converge and culminate in the agape. Thus, in the Mass, the center of creation and of the redemptive Incarna-tion, the Word incarnate is the mediator and the Spirit the fulfillment. In the Mass as in the Trinity all issues from the Father who is not manifested directly but through the Son and Holy Spirit, and it is to him that all returns through his word and in his Spirit.

THE SPIRITUALITY OF THE DESERT*

Quae est ista quae ascendit per desertum?
(What is that coming up out of the desert?)

Song of Songs 3:6

BIBLICAL DESERT

A. *Desert of Exodus*

STOPPING PLACES from spring to spring, from the Red Sea to Canaan. Perfect period: forty years. Miracles like mirages: quail and manna, split rock and water pouring forth.... Wandering, seeking, waiting. Hope for a land, a kingdom, a Messiah.... Eschatology like the horizon ahead of the caravan. Harshness of life accepted because of hope. For Moses, the initiator, desire will not become reality. He is to die on Mount Nebo. Yahweh, like Israel, lives in a tent: the wandering God of a wandering people. From the burnt rocks of Sinai comes the Torah. The altars are of unhewn stone: desert worship. Adoration of the only One, dazzled amazement before his transcendence. 'Listen Israel, you have but one God.'

---

* ©Casterman s.a. éditeurs, Tournai-Paris, 1967.

166

The prophets, after the foundation of the kingdom, of cities, and of peace, will turn their yearning toward the time of Exodus and toward the desert of Exodus, when God had no house and his people no home.   Were Solomon's barbarian luxury and the Cedars of Sidon worth as much as the rocks heaped up between two desert spaces by wandering worshippers?

B.   *Desert of the Precursor*

Nothing is mentioned of him except *exultatio in utero, vox in deserto...*   Child, adolescent, young man?... He flees to regions beyond the Jordan, dressed like a nomad, eating nothing, hungering only for him who is to come. He has only to decrease: his West conditions the other's East. Among this people who know no sacraments, he prepares the way to the sacrament. A kind of brotherhood is formed around the just and fearsome prophet, precursor of the supreme judgement. Embryo of a desert community born of a renewing water. Even Christ came there, last and first; He who ends and begins; He who separates John's disciples from John and John perhaps within himself. 'Are you the One who is to come?' The water of repentance becomes the water of the trinitarian Epiphany and the messianic proclamation.

C.   *Desert of the Temptation*

Christ is thrust by the spirit—who overshadowed his mother and whom he himself will send, another Paraclete— thrust into the desert. Forty days that recall the forty years. Exodus ends in this encounter between the Son of Jacob and the other angel: the Temptor. No manna: the calcined rocks he refused to change into bread. No miracles: weak like a man, he will not throw himself down from the roof of the Temple. No concupiscence for land or kingdoms. What was essential to the desert of exodus is all that remains in the desert of temptation: adoration and abandonment to God alone.

CHRISTIAN DESERT

Christianity spreading first to port-cities and towns—Jerusalem, Antioch, Ephesus, Corinth, Rome—reaches the solitary places before it reaches the countryside. Paul, Anthony, Hilarion, Pachomius, Paphnutius...become anchorites and then cenobites of the Desert. The life of solitude is covered with *lauras*. A substitute for martyrdom, asceticism drenches these men, these women. Penance, however, is not enough for them: they examine Scripture, recite the Psalms, meditate. Evagrius will extract a desert mysticism: solitude in prayer such that the one who prays does not even know he prays,...recollection of the whole being within the interior image where God appears. Nakedness of sense, intelligence, mind. The monastic orders, Basilians in the East, Benedictines in the West, were born from a period when their founders lived in solitude: Egypt and Subiaco. Francis of Assisi withdrew to Alverno and even Saint Ignatius to Manresa.

The great orders will consider themselves extensions of the desert destined to recall the sanctity typical of the desert Fathers (great influence of Cassian and of the *Vitae patrum* on the entire development of monastic life). Particularly Carmelites, who see themselves descended from the elianic solitary places, and the Carthusians, planted by Saint Bruno in the solitude of the Alps, extend in a more communal form the half-cenobitic anchoretic life of numerous hermits of ancient times.

DESERT-SIGN

Endless walking across the unchanging plains of alpha, rock, and sand, where mirages vanish. There are stagnant wells, and the water so long desired leaves thirst. Desert patience of one who is called, already sharing the solitude of God, called to a vision which will make him forget all things previously seen. Harshness, severity of forms and lines. The accidental is worn away by the essential: God is sufficient.

But yet, quiet calm of evenings, nights under the stars: ordered chance. Grace, too, sketches with our daily gestures the shapes of order to the wonder of the saints. The oasis, water, and shade, like visitations of the Spirit: the garden of Eden, that only needs be crossed...and the walking begins again, and the devouring light, and the solitude, and the calcination. The horizon's perfect circle, in the desert as on the sea: nowhere else but within his presence. Dazzled *extasis* before the only One: God is One.

SPIRITUALITY

Detachment, breaking off, renunciation. Harshness, too, and monotony of weeks, months, years without change. The relentless call of God has left only the taste for the essential and the essential is concealed. Daily life is filled with tedium, danger.... If there are joys, a secret urgency recalls that they must be crossed over. The night of the senses, of the intelligence, of the mind might well be called the desert, according to a Ruysbroeckian image. Everything is marked with intensity: temptations and disgust, fears and the feeling of emptiness and absence. There is only exodus and no *extasis*, and the Sole One is perceived through solitude apart from him rather than through solitude with him. Now the human caravan is hardly felt except as bondage. Yet, exodus has no meaning except through the Promised Land, and this absence is the reverse and the annunciation of the Presence. Fidelity to the monotonous walking in a calcined desert is the act of faith that God asks: bare faith that, without knowing it, includes hope and is identified with perfect love in perfect solitude; faith which is anticipation, already possession, imperceptible to consciousness, of the ecstatic unity with the Sole One.

Renunciation in this life of the experience of this nuptial and adoring love can be, according to the law of substitution, the inducement and the entrance into that Love of those who—called to the faith in the deserts of Arabia and spread out like the crescent of the moon from the Gobi desert to the desert of the Rio de Oro, in the image of their mother Hagar driven into the desert with Ishmael whose prayer brought forth living water—continue to be deprived of the sense and the joys of this Presence and this Love.

THE SONG OF SONGS

The whole universe is less than the day
when the Song of Songs was given to Israel,
for all Biblical songs come from the Holy One,
but the Song of Songs is the Holy of Holies.

Rabbi Akiba

THESE SONGS OF LOVE which are perhaps nuptial, perhaps not—the Beloved prefers her shepherd to Solomon's harem—are placed within a traditional and imaginary dramatic framework (Solomon and the Sulamite) perhaps with opposition between the odalisk and the Beloved: Hazan—with burning yet chaste love.

The stratagems of love, alternating scenes and rhythms, presence, absence, flight, return, the hind and the fawn. And the images: night and noon, mountain and desert, vine, garden, and inner room. And the dancing perhaps (Hazan) of the Beloved leading up to the *extasis* and the cry, the oracle:

> *Love is strong as death;*
> *Jealousy is cruel as sheol;*
> *Its flashes are flame,*
> *The fire of God....* (8:6)

There is only one *love*, substantial sign and substance.

These stratagems: his stratagems. He invites Israel—the Church and myself—and (like the Lover from the Beloved) is hidden from Israel, from the Church and from me.

In the morning burning, dry and solitary, in the night of dereliction and anguish, in the morning when sprinkled with dew he looks through the lattice work of phenomena.

More so than in Plato, beauty leads to his Beauty. Without dialectics, without passing through numbers; suddenly creative intuition, without the mediation of consciousness, is grafted on unconsciousness. But it is a leap which crossed over death (or *extasis*, another death), from the I to the thou, from the thou of love to the thou of adoration. 'O thou more mir; than myself, who alone art'—love within the mystery:

> *Durus ut mors dilectio.*
> *Love is strong as death.*

SERMONS ON THE BLESSED VIRGIN [18]

MARY MOTHER OF THE WORD INCARNATE.

CHRIST IS THE CENTER of Creation. He is the 'first born of creatures.' God desired the world only as the setting for life, man for life, and Christ as God-Man.

Christ is not separable from his Mother. 'He made himself what we are so that we might become what he is' (Saint Irenaeus).

If Christ is consubstantial with the Father and the Spirit, he is also consubstantial with human nature through Mary. He is totally turned toward the Trinity in order to give praise and toward man in order to divinize him.

Through his Mother he takes root in the world.

Mary, the human source of Christ, was desired from the beginning—as for Christ, the world was desired by Mary.

The preparation for this coming of Mary: 'I was conceived from all Eternity.'

Man appears, man sins, man is punished. But the annunciation of the Redeemer can be understood through the annunciation of the woman, co-redeemer and victorious over sin.

173

The people of God: Israel, the prophets, the people called in Abraham. Abraham's response: 'Here am I' for the departure and for the immolation of his son. Then the promise of a posterity which will include the Virgin of Israel, prefigured by the Jewish holy women and sung of in the Song of Songs.

In the heart of Israel, a family is chosen: Joachim and Anna (the prayer in the Protoevanglium of James).

And Mary immaculate in her conception appears full of graces. In her, no tendency toward evil, no sin, that is, no refusal of God, nothing in her nature weighed down. She is transparent to the Spirit.

Her youth consecrated to God in poverty (real poverty, God was enough for her; she left the house of her father in order to be in the house of the Father, the temple). She is a virgin (a thing unheard of in Israel) even in her marriage. Every woman in Israel dreamed of motherhood. Mary loves Joseph; her love is a transparent gift, but in absolute virginity, for Mary does not labor for the perpetuation of earthly life. She labors only for God.

She is contemplative. She reads the law and the prophets. She is wholly the silent and burning expectation of the Messiah. She is adoration of the holiness of God and she is expectation in eager hope of the Messiah.

Each of us has an irreplaceable vocation. God expects of us something which no one can do in our place: to be like Mary, solely expectation, the immense desire for God. It is through Mary that Christ takes root in this world.

Stages of this maternity:

The Annunciation: Trembling Mary receives the angel. She utters the greatest word that a religious person can utter: 'Behold the handmaid', which answers to Abraham's 'Here I am.' At that moment the Word is made flesh that it might dwell among us. Scripture customarily indicates the divine presence by a cloud. This cloud is the sign of the third Person of the Holy Trinity, he who is the culmination of this great outpouring of God.

It is in the Spirit that the Father and the Word are ONE. It is this Spirit which penetrates Mary. She was sinless, utterly porous to the Spirit. She is transpierced. Every fiber belongs to the spirit. No nuptial union is comparable to this fusion, more intimate and substantial than Eucharistic communion.

The Visitation. Mary cannot contain her joy. *Magnificat:* one of the highest expressions of praise. The canticle of the poor, the satisfying of a soul full of desire. She recalls Abraham.... Spiritual writers of the seventeenth century prayed: 'O Jesus living in Mary'—especially in the season of Advent.

The Word is so silent that he is at first unspeaking and unmoving. Even Joseph does not know. Mary is the only one to know, the only one to adore, to contemplate, to love. There is only one single Christian and the Church has already been born. Already Mary 'ponders all these things in her heart' (Luke 2:19). This Messiah has become within her— under the glorious overshadowing of the Spirit—the Son of Man.

Christmas. Mary standing in joy—as she will stand later in sorrow. Mary gives birth without pain, without tears, in poverty and in joy.

Nazareth. A mother and a teacher. Mary was in a real way the teacher of Jesus, for 'the Word reduced to the form of a slave' was to learn his maternal language. She forms his sensibility, his thought, his knowledge of experience. She teaches him to pray (throughout all his life Jesus will say Jewish prayers).

Mary's motherhood has given its ultimate meaning to all motherhood. Every woman who is a mother resembles Mary in some way. Like Mary, she gives her life, this sacred thing which is beyond us; like Mary, she prostrates herself before the secret of God; like Mary, she forms the soul.

Mothers, be like this mother so that your sons may be other Christs.

MARY CO-REDEEMER AT THE CROSS.

Substitution: John in the place of Jesus. Mary's heart is opened to the dimensions of the world. This substitution signifies the substitution of humanity, of the Church for Jesus.

'It is good for you that I go away' (John 16:7). Jesus passes from the mortal Christ to the immortal Christ. This difficult passage from the visible Christ to the invisible Christ was made a reality by Mary on Calvary. From that time on she knew herself to be the mother of the Church which she brought forth in sorrow.

Her heart was torn. No greater sorrow for a mother than seeing her Son tortured to death.

Passion and compassion truly complement each other. Mary was the foremost of those who suffered with him, of those stigmatized in heart and soul. She gave definite meaning to suffering. All sorrow, which is the clash of the finite against the infinite, must be a moving forward: passing from one ideal of life to a higher ideal.

There are some persons who are degraded by suffering, because it is crushing for those who fail in their mission of suffering. Philosophy is unable to resolve the problem of suffering, but in Christ all suffering has found its absolute meaning.

Easter morning and its joy are the transubstantiation of the sorrow of Good Friday when Christ took on himself all the suffering of men.

'Jesus will be in agony until the end of the world.'

There is something lacking in Christ's passion as long as one member of the Church does not share in the compassion.

Mary gives meaning to compassion and a creative sense to suffering.

If we suffer with her and with Jesus, no suffering can be in vain—not merely our going beyond, but God may ask us to take upon ourselves the suffering of others, at the foot of the Cross, with a pierced heart, dying with Jesus.

MARY MOTHER OF THE MYSTICAL BODY.

Mary knew that the tomb would not hold Jesus, that Christ had entered a totally different life. The Resurrection means for Christ the entry into a totally new life. His divine power, which was limited in his earthly life, becomes immediate for every creature. He is risen for us in order to communicate his divine life. He is simultaneously in the glory of the Father and among us.

After the Resurrection his Incarnation remains infinitely mysterious. He is hidden from human eyes, concealed within the Father as he was concealed within Mary before his birth.

The Ascension puts an end to the human visions of Christ. He remains perceptible only through faith.

Saint Augustine tells us that Mary is the Mother of God, of his humanity. Mary did not bring forth the glorious Christ, but she is a partner in his glorious life. Mary did not remain bodily in the tomb. She had shared his sufferings, it was right for her to share in his glory.

Mary—partner in the Resurrection through her body.

Mother of God already inseparable from Christ in heavenly glory.

Christ continues to act in this world. Maternally, Mary draws the universe toward her Son. She is in glory, she contemplates the Trinity. Further, she shares in the Trinitarian movement.

But this holiness is not individualistic. Only one body, only one cathedral with Christ as keystone. Mary on the other shore shows the way. She shares in the eternal generation of the Word by the Father, in the breathing forth of the Spirit towards the Father and the Son. Mary is a partner in the glory of Christ in her very innermost substance.

After the Ascension, Christ has not deserted the world. He is present: really, in the Mystical Body and sensibly, in the Eucharist.

Tradition tells us that Mary lived with John in Ephesus. She was present at the Masses of John and received Communion, and her faith penetrated the mysteries of the

Eucharist.   The interchanges of these Communions were
lengthened by meditation.   She remains the Mother of Christ
in the Eucharistic state.

Through Mary, eternally woman and mother, we can go to
Christ.   She can give us that desire, that annihilation of self
so that we may receive Christ like her.

Christ = the ultimate self-annihilation before the Creator
= the highest praise.

But Christ is always priest—this mediation essentially
constitutes him.   'He made himself what we are so that we
might become what he is.'

Per ipsum, cum ipso, et in ipso (Through him, with him,
and in him).

Mary's vocation is inseparable from Christ's.   She
continues to love Christ in us.

No one has the knowledge of the Mystical Body as she
has.   With each of us, 'members, humanity in addition to
Christ' she experiences a spiritual motherhood.   Her
mediation has a double quality.   She makes our prayers rise
up to God like the double ladder of the Old Testament.
Through her everything rises to Christ and to the Holy
Trinity.

But she gives more than she receives.   There is no grace
which flows to humanity without passing through Christ, thus
through Mary indissolubly united to Christ.

But she gives not only graces but the grace which is a
unique gift: the Spirit.

She possesses the Spirit more than anyone, she overflows
with the Holy Spirit to whom she always says: 'Here I am.'
Let us too ask for the Holy Spirit, the Paraclete, Love.

THE SPIRITUALITY OF MARY.

Saint Catherine of Siena: 'He who knows in Truth, burns
with Love.'

We must know Mary in Truth.   History tells us few things
about her.   The restraint of the Gospels.

It is through meditation that we can know her.

Let us meditate on the Gospel from the point of view of Mary—to know her and to praise her.

The Magnificat is a canticle of praise which we must make our own. We should not disdain simple devotions, like the Rosary, the Psalter of the Virgin—a hundred fifty Hail Marys, a hundred fifty psalms.

The Hail Mary contains what is essential in devotion to Mary. But the Rosary is also a meditation, a way of reliving the mysteries of Jesus and Mary's motherhood in relation to these mysteries. Congregations and guilds for the recitation of the Rosary are excellent if they 'burn with love.' The cult of Mary must never be separated from Christ and the Holy Trinity.

We must go through Mary to find her Son.

Love her like a son. Find again the ways of childhood. In all our trials, spiritual dryness and external hardships, turn to her.

Loving is not enough. We must imitate her. Imitate her abandonment to God, her humility, her silence, her holiness, her adoration.

'Behold the handmaid of the Lord,' the heart of Mary's attitude, the heart of the religious attitude.

A person is religious when he abandons himself in adoration. This is difficult in moments of sorrow when one rises up against Providence, agitated by ideas of hatred, of vengeance in unrelieved darkness.

Mary is so humble that she never sought to play any role in the newly formed Church. She never pointed to herself, or attempted to say 'I'.

We civilized Europeans practice introspection, we study our sins, we have fits of scrupulosity, we contemplate ourselves in our growth, we display our joy, we analyze ourselves.

But we should look at God alone.

Mary knew how to transform the most ordinary human things—washing, marketing, sewing—into divine things. She led the life of an ordinary woman, of a poor woman. Nothing external would set her apart from her neighbors. Holiness is the *transfiguration of daily life.*

Silence: Mary said little else than her Magnificat.

Mary never told her story to any one (the mania of spiritual writers to do their biographies!).

Adoration: God is the sole necessity. Everything else is a way of reaching God in her.

The Trinity is in us in so far as we do not exile it by a tragic refusal to love. Do we know what this means?

Mary is the mediatrix. Christ is the way. We must be raised up from his humanity to his Trinity.

'To Jesus through Mary.'

From Mary to Christ and the Trinity,

the family of love.

THE TRINITY: AN ESSAY IN THE LIGHT OF PERSONALISM*
Paris, 20 September, 1957

THE REVELATION of the Old and particularly the New Testament has shown to the world how deeply man is person—soul immortal, irreplaceable, priceless, in the very eyes of the Creator—and how deeply God especially is persons—the Trinity. Slowly there has developed in regard to the Trinity, to the personality of Christ, and to the value of man himself a Christian personalism not yet fully aware of its philosophical basis. During the past century and particularly in the twentieth century, personalism has developed as a system (emphasizing freedom, the incomparability of individuals, the reciprocity of consciences, principally in love).

The human person, in the image of the divine Persons, seems constituted by two essential poles: ipseity and communicability. Normally the one grows with the other (the deepest friendships among the most personal beings and among the strongest personalities). One must be in order to give. The more one is, the more one is capable of giving: *Bonum diffusivum sui.*

Now, nothing could be finite in God without absolute contradiction. The alterity of each divine Person in relation to the others exceeds the alterity of any other being, infinitely.

181

This very alterity to the infinite degree is constitutive of unity to the infinite degree. A dynamic unity which is expressed by a curve going from the unfathomable God, apophatic to the maximum, whose revealed name is Father, the *source* Godhead according to Saint John Damascene, to the person whom Scripture calls at once Son and Word, the intelligibility of impenetrable Being. The Word which issues from the silence of the Father (Saint Ignatius of Antioch) finds its ultimate point of completion and return in the Trinitarian cycle, manifested in the eternal instant: 'The monad is manifested in triad without acretion and the triad is gathered into monad without reduction.' (Denis of Alexandria, replying to a lost letter of Pope Denis.) We might say metaphorically that the infinite speed of this incomparable internal dynamism is the equivalent of infinite stability.

Far from being opposed to each other in God, the One and the Three mutually require each other. Without plurality of persons, there could be no person: no Father without the Word (who is *a Patre*) no Spirit without the Father and the Word, *procedens ab utroque tanquam ab uno principio* (Council of Florence).

Inversely without unity, there would be only triplicity of Gods and no God.

We should try to avoid using the expression 'divine family' which the early Fathers would certainly have anathematized. The discovery of the full personality of each person as basis for all forms of spirituality, particularly of Christian families, is one of God's gifts in our time; but this discovery must not veil the infrangible unity of the divine essence. It would mean returning to paganism.

FOOTNOTES

1. Inseparable union.

2. See Chap. II, note 1.

3. Eph 1:23.

4. Śankara (ca. 788-820): southern Indian philosopher and partisan of pure non-dualism.

5. Tauler, a German mystic (1300-1361) and disciple of Eckhart.

6. *I-Ching, The Book of Changes:* a work of divination dating from the eighth or seventh century BC.

7. A *lakh* is the equivalent of one hundred thousand, and a *crore* that of ten million.

8. A certain affinity with the language of Teilhard de Chardin must not conceal the originality of Monchanin's own thought, which is centered on the mystery of the Trinity: *alpha* and *omega*. For a less technical version of the following essay, see: *L'abbé Jules Monchanin,* 'Formes, Vie, et Pensee,' pp. 162-175. For a comparison between Teilhard and Monchanin, see H. de Lubac, *Images de l'abbé Monchanin,* pp. 119-151.

9. Jean Guitton, *Le Temps et l'éternité chez Plotin et Saint-Augustin* (Paris: Boivin et Cie., 1933).

10. Edouard Le Roy, *La Pensée intuitive* (Paris: Boivin et Cie., 1929); *L'Exigence idéaliste et le fait de l'évolution* (Paris: Boivin et Cie., 1927).

11. Cf. *Time and the Eternal*, pp. 134-6.

12. 'For God, deified creation is not an unfolding in time but a reality completed in the infinite tension of the Trinity. Thus, absolute Circumincession in the Trinity is relative-absolute in deification, and it is the same tension of communion both among the divine Persons in themselves and in the temporal projection (*a parte mundi*) of their relationships: keystone of the Trinity as well as of the creation in fullness in the Mystical Body'— *Monchanin*.

13. 'On creation *ab aeterno.* In itself creation does not imply an absolute beginning, but signifies an intemporal relationship between the eternal and the temporal, a relationship of absolute dependence. This problem of creation *in tempore* or *ab aeterno* is not a metaphysical one, but a relgious one: the interpretation of Genesis. St Thomas in his short work *De aeternitate mundi adversus murmurantes* defends the philosophical possibility of creation *ab aeterno.* He rejects it as a reality because of Genesis 1:1: *In principio creavit Deus caelum et terram* (In the beginning God created heaven and earth). Creation *in tempore* was defined as a matter of

faith by the Council of Vienne. But what does *in principio* mean? Should we not see it in terms of an origin conceived of from an imaginative perspective and in order to envelope in temporal imagery an intemporal relationship which cannot be grasped by unsubtle minds? Relating Genesis 1:1 to John 1:1, several Fathers of the Church have understood 'in the Logos,' symbolically. Exegetically the problem is not clear cut. The Council of Vienne defined creation in time in opposition to pantheism and not in opposition to a creation *ab aeterno* which would place the world *ab aeterno* in time. An absolute beginning is unrepresentable, if not unthinkable, to us. It even seems to introduce in a dishonest way a time anterior to time. The mind is instead drawn to the idea of a creation coextensive with creative power *ab aeterno, in aeternum'—Monchanin.*

14. Cf. *The Trinity: An Essay in the Light of Personalism*, pp.181-2. There is no personality except through integration into the Mystical Body.

15. *Pleroma*, fullness. Cf. *La Théologie de Saint Paul*, by F. Prat, I, pp. 352-355, Beauchesne ed.

16. *Dictionnaire apologétique.*

17. 'Yet, see Rousselot: *L'intellectualism de Saint Thomas et le problème de l'amour au Moyen Age'—Monchanin.*

18. In both France and India Father Monchanin preached a great deal and gave many retreats for persons of quite diverse social and intellectual backgrounds. These retreats, although carefully thought out, were not written down for presentation. The following extracts or résumés of Sermons on the Blessed Virgin, which were transcribed by persons present at his retreats, and later revised by Father Monchanin himself, constitute an important theological and spiritual synthesis based on scripture and tradition.

GLOSSARY

Advaita—Vedāntic non-dualism, the non-two, fundamental to Indian religious and philosophical thought. *Advaita* denies the separateness of any aspect of reality from the impersonal oneness of *Brahman.*

*Advaitin—*a believer in *advaita.*

*Apavāda—*The successive elimination of *upādhis,* i.e. those determining and limiting forms imposed on the Self through ignorance by which one is bound to earthly life. The goal of *apavāda* is *Nirguna-Brahman,* the absolute, the unique reality.

*Apophatism—*Negative theology, emphasizing the transcendence of God; a *via negationis* through which the soul proceeds mostly by rejection and negation.

*Ashram—*A hermitage, a type of monastery; a place of retreat for a colony of disciples. It can also refer to any one of the four stages of life: the celibate student stage, the married householder stage, the stage of retirement and contemplation, the stage of religious mendicancy.

*Atman—*The self or soul. It also denotes the Supreme Soul, which, according to *Advaita Vedānta,* is one with the individual soul; the innermost essence of each individual; also, the Supreme Universal Self.

*Avatāra—*The descent, incarnation, of a deity.

*Bhakti—*Religious devotion, specifically love directed toward a personal deity. *Bhaktimārga:* the way of *bhakti.*

*Bodhi—*The state of enlightenment attained by a Buddhist after practising the Eightfold Path and achieving salvation; intellectual illumination; perfect understanding of truth.

*Bodhisattva—*A being whose nature (*sattva*) is pure knowledge; a being that, through compassion, refrains from entering *nirvāna,* in order to lead others on the path of salvation.

Brahmā—In the *Vedas*: Supreme Reality, Cosmic Energy; the sacred, the divine, the absolute; the Creator God, the first Person of the Hindu Trinity (the other two being *Vishnu* and *Śiva*).

Brahman—The holy power; life monad; one-without-a-second; self.

Brāhman or *Brāhmin*—The priestly *caste*, the highest of the four great *castes* of Indian society. Their primary duty is the study and teaching of the *Vedas* and the performance of religious ceremonies.

Brāhmo-Samāj—A theistic movement in India founded in the nineteenth century by Rammohan Roy. It was noted for its monotheism and strong belief in social and political reform. See also, Chapter III, note 16, p. 109.

Caste—A hereditary, closed social class. There are four great *castes*, each having many subdivisions and its own rules and rites: the *Brāhmans*, or priests, said, in the *Vedas*, to have sprung from the head of *Brahmā*; the *Kshatriyas*, or soldiers, from his arms; the *Vaiśyas*, farmers and merchants, from his belly; and the *Śudras*, or laborers, from his feet. The *Pariahs*, or untouchables, are variously considered as a low *caste* or as excluded from the *caste* system.

Chakra—The wheel, a disk representing the sun and sovereignty.

Chakravartin—Kings of the *Vidyadhara*, beings analogous to men but endowed with magical powers. Also, a universal sovereign, ideal ruler.

Dharma—Righteousness, the inner principle of religion; often translated as religion. The word is also used in a more general sense as duty. Although its primary meaning is the norm of religious and ritual life, it also includes private and public behavior and social relationships.

Guru—Spiritual teacher.

Jñāna—Spiritual knowledge. Jñānamārga: the way of spiritual knowledge.

Karma—Action in general; duty; specifically ritual worship. *Karmamārga*: the way of ritual.

Kavi—The ochre-colored robe commonly worn by Indian monks.

Kevala—The alone, the absolute. *Kaivalya* is the final state of salvation, the absolute release of the embodied soul (*jiva*) from all the entanglements with inanimate matter (*ajiva*).

Līlā—The divine play or game. Creation is often spoken of as the *līlā* of God. As a philosophical term *līlā* (the relative) is the correlative of *nitya* (the changeless, absolute).

Mahātmā—A great soul, a person deserving of reverence for his wisdom, holiness and selflessness.

Mahāyāna—The Great Vehicle, one of the two great schools of Buddhism.

Mantra—Holy Sanskrit text; also the sacred formula or invocation used in the repetition of God's name (*japa*).

Māyā—In general, the illusion-creating power of a demon or a god. The cosmic illusion, or the powerful force that creates the illusion, that the phenomenal world is real; ignorance obscuring the vision of God; also used to denote attachment.

Mokśa—Liberation, release, or final emancipation, one of the four ends of human pursuit.

Nirguna-Brahman—A term used to describe the Absolute. Literally: *Brahman* without attributes; the absolute, the unique reality.

Nirvāna—The blowing out or extinction of life; reunion with *Brahman*. Final absorption in *Brahman* or the All-pervading Reality, by the annihilation of passions, desires, and the individual ego.

Pāli—The sacred language of India. An Indic language which became the language of the Buddhist canon. Today it is the liturgical and scholarly language of Hīnayāna Buddhism.

Para-Nirguna-Brahman—Supreme knowledge.

Pariah—A member of a low *caste* of Southern India and Burma. An untouchable; one who does not belong to any of the chief *castes*.

Parināma—Real transformation of cause into effect; God becoming creature.

Pipal—In India, a fig tree, also called the bo tree, renowned for its great size and longevity. It is to be distinguished from the banyan by the lack of prop roots. The tree is held sacred by Buddhists because it is believed that Gautama received his divine illumination under one of them.

Pipāla—The bodhi tree which was the tree of Buddha's illumination.

Pudgala—(A Buddhist term) Primary matter, composed of minute atoms and having characteristics of odor, color, taste, tangibility.

Ramakrishna Mission—A neo-Hinduist society established to spread the message of Ramakrishna Paramahamsa (1834-1886) whose belief that all the religious forms of Hinduism are only aspects of a same truth also encompassed non-Hindu religions such as Islam and Christianity.

Rāmāyana—The great Sanskrit epic recounting the story of *Rāma*, one of the incarnations of Vishnu.

Saccidānanda—*Brahman* as Being (*sat*), Consciousness (*cit*), Bliss (*ānanda*).

Sādhu—A holy man; a Hindu mendicant ascetic; a wandering

monk living alone or with others and belonging to any religious sect. The *Sādhu* is usually distinguished by his saffron robe.

Śaivasiddhanta—The body of Śivite wisdom, a large body of knowledge in Tamil (thirteenth century) which postulates the existence of three great principles: the Master (*Śiva*), the Bond or Link (*paga,* matter), the Soul.

Samsāra—The world; the endless round of being.

Sannyāsi—One who renounces all to live as a hermit. A Hindu monk; today usually synonymous with *sādhu.*

Sāri—A woman's ankle-length garment made of one piece and forming both a skirt and shoulder covering.

Shantivanam—Grove of peace (*shanti*: peace), the name which Monchanin and Le Saux gave to their hermitage.

Śiva—The Destroyer God, the third member of the Hindu Trinity, the *Trimurti* (the Three Forms), the other two being *Brahmā* and *Vishnu.*

Śloka—The verse form of Sanskrit epics similar to a distich.

Stūpa—A type of mound or tower constructed of earth, brick, or stone serving as a reliquary or commemorative monument.

Swami—Lord; a spiritual teacher; a title of monks belonging to the *Vedānta* school; a member of a Hindu religious order; in general, a title of respect.

Tahśildar—A magistrate or district tax-collector.

Tantra (adj., *Tantric*)—A religious philosophy where the Divine Mother or Power is the Ultimate Reality; the scriptures that deal with this philosophy.

Tao—The unitary first principle from which all things come; the eternal order of the universe; in Confucianism: the path of virtuous conduct.

Triloka—The three worlds: heaven, earth, hell.

Upādhi—Limiting, conditioning attributes; a term in *Vedāntic* philosophy denoting the limitations imposed on the Self through ignorance by which one is bound to worldly life.

Upanishads—Fundamental philosophical and religious texts of Brahmanism dealing with broad philosophical problems such as the nature of man, the universe, etc.

Vaishnava—Literally: follower of Vishnu. A dualistic sect, a member of the same, worshipping Vishnu in any of his forms or incarnations.

Veda[s]—The most sacred Hindu scriptures.

Vedānta—One of the six systems (*darshanas*) of orthodox Hindu philosophy, formulated by Vyāsa; also, sections of the *Upanishads*, poetic dialogues commenting on the *Vedas*; a systematization of orthodox Brahmanic philosophy of the *Upanishads*.

Vishnu—The Preserver God, the Second Person of the Hindu Trinity (the other two being *Brahmā* and *Śiva*); the personal God of the *Vaishnavas*.

Viśista-Advaita—The philosophy of qualified non-dualism (*advaita* with attributes).

Yin-Yang—In Chinese cosmology, the complementary forces that produce all that comes into being; the female and male principles respectively. *Yin* (the female) stands for the negative principle in nature: passivity, depth, darkness, coldness, etc. *Yang* (the male) stands for the positive principle in nature: activity, height, light, heat. They are the fundamental modalities of the *Tao*.

Yoga—The union of the individual soul with the Universal Soul; also an ascetic practice or method of contemplation seeking to liberate the individual from the wholly illusory world of phenomena.

A SELECTED BIBLIOGRAPHY

WORKS BY MONCHANIN

'L'amitié et l'amour: de la solitude à Dieu,' *Médecine et Adolescence.* Lyon: Lavandier, 1936.

'Apophatisme et Apavada,' *Entretiens 1955*, Publications de l'Institut français d'Indologie, No. 4. Pondichéry, 1956.

'Biologie et morale sexuelles,' *Questions relatives à la sexualité.* Lyon: Laboratoires Lumière, 1930.

'La caste aux Indes,' *Cahiers des A.L.M.*, 1939, No. 1.

'Constantes de la Chine,' *Cahiers des A.L.M.*, 1939, No. 2.

'La crise de l'espérance,' *Eglise Vivante*, 1949 No. 1; and *France-Asie*, 1952, décembre, No. 79.

'Culture et loisirs,' *Chronique sociale de France*, 1938, 15 juin.

De l'esthétique à la mystique, 2e édition. Préface par Pierre Emmanuel. Paris-Tournai: Casterman, 1967.

Ecrits spirituels. Présentation d'Edouard Duperray. Paris: Centurion, 1965.

'L'église et la pensée indienne,' *Bulletin des Missions*, 1936, No. 4.

'Enigmes dravidiennes,' *Cahiers du Sud:* "Approches de L'Inde," 1949.

'L'espèce humaine: essai de synthèse,' *Hérédité et races.* Lyon: Lavandier, 1929-30.

'Essai de spiritualité missionnaire,' *Eglise Vivante*, 1949, No. 3.

'Essai de synthèse: santé, sagesse, sainteté,' *Médecine et Education*. Lyon: Lavandier, 1933-34.

'Expansion du bouddhisme en Chine,' *Bulletin de l'association catholique chinoise du Sud-Est de la France*, 1931, 7 décembre.

'Formes, vie et pensée,' *Formes, vie et pensée*. Lyon: Lavandier, 1931-33.

'Hindouisme,' *Bulletin des facultés catholiques de Lyon*, 1946, juillet-décembre.

'Hommage à Mahatma Gandhi,' *Bulletin des Missions*, 1948, No. 3.

'L'Inde d'aujourd'hui, *Cahiers des A.L.M.*, 1947, juillet.

'L'Inde et la contemplation,' *Dieu Vivant*, 1945, No. 3.

'L'Inde et l'esprit de l'Ancien Testament,' *Bulletin de l'association Ad Lucam*, 1963.

'Islam et Christianisme, *Bulletin des Missions*, 1938, No. 1.

'Jalons pour une théologie missionnaire: corps mystique et missiologie,' *Bulletin du Cercle Saint-Jean-Baptiste*, 1953, décembre.

'Le monachisme et l'Inde,' *Eglise Vivante*, 1952, No. 2.

'La pensée de Shri Aurobindo,' *Eglise Vivante*, 1952, No. 2.

'Perspectives missionnaires,' La revue *SAM*, 1939, Nos. 41-3.

'Pouja hindoue et sacrifice chrétien,' *Bulletin du Cercle Saint-Jean-Baptiste*, février, 1957.

'The Quest of the Absolute,' *Indian Culture and the Fullness of Christ*. Madras: The Catholic Centre, 1956.

'Religions et civilisations indiennes,' *Bulletin d'Histoire des Religions: Recherches de science religieuse*, 1949.

'Rythmes humains: les rythmes de la vie de l'esprit,' *Les rythmes et la vie*. Lyon: Lavandier, 1930-31.

'Spiritualité chinoise,' *Cahiers des A.L.M.*, 1939, no. 3.

'La spiritualité du désert,' *Dieu Vivant*, 1945, No. 1.

'Le temps selon l'hindouisme et le christianisme,' *Dieu Vivant*, 1949, No. 14.

'Théologie et mystique du Saint-Esprit,' *Dieu Vivant*, 1949, No. 23.

'Yoga et hésychasme,' *Entretiens 1955*, Publications de l'Institut français d'Indologie, No. 4. Pondichéry, 1956.

IN COLLABORATION WITH HENRI LE SAUX OSB

A Benedictine Ashram, revised edition. Douglas: Times Press, 1964.

Ermites du Saccidânanda, 2e édition. Paris-Tournai: Casterman, 1957.

'L'heure de l'Inde,' *Eglise Vivante*, 1955, No. 1.

'Le Malentendu,' *Eglise Vivante*, 1955, No. 2.

ON MONCHANIN

[Duperray, Edouard.] *L'abbé Jules Monchanin*. Paris-Tournai: Casterman, 1960.

Emmanuel, Pierre. *Qui est cet homme? ou le singulier universel*. Paris: Egloff, 1947. (Emmanuel's autobiography has a short section on Monchanin.)

'La vocation de Jules Monchanin,' *Bulletin du Cercle Saint Jean-Baptiste*, 1967, février.

Le Saux, Henri. 'Le père Monchanin, Swami Parama Arubi Anandam,' *La Vie spirituelle*, 1958, janvier.

[Le Saux, Henri.] *Swami Parama Arubi Anandam (Fr. Jules Monchanin) 1895-1957: A Memorial*. Tiruchirapalli, Saccidānanda Ashram, 1959.

de Lubac, Henri. *Images de l'abbé Monchanin*. Paris: Aubier, 1967.

Lyon, Jean. 'Vie et mort de l'abbé Monchanin,' *Promesses*, Noël, 1961.

CISTERCIAN PUBLICATIONS

THE CISTERCIAN FATHERS SERIES

THE WORKS OF BERNARD OF CLAIRVAUX

Treatises I (Apologia to Abbot William, On Precept and Dispensation) CF 1

On the Song of Songs I CF 4

On the Song of Songs II CF 7

Treatises II (The Steps of Humility, On Loving God)CF 13

Five Books on Consideration CF 37

THE WORKS OF WILLIAM OF ST THIERRY

On Contemplating God, Prayer, Meditations CF 3

Exposition on the Song of Songs CF 6

The Enigma of Faith CF 9

*The Golden Epistle CF 12

THE WORKS OF AELRED OF RIEVAULX

Treatises I (On Jesus at the Age of Twelve, Rule for a Recluse, The Pastoral Prayer) CF 2

Spiritual Friendship CF 5

THE WORKS OF GUERRIC OF IGNY

Liturgical Sermons
two volumes CF 8, CF 32

OTHERS

The Letters of Adam of Perseigne I CF 21

The Way of Love CF 16

THE CISTERCIAN STUDIES SERIES

CISTERCIAN STUDIES

The Cistercian Spirit: A Symposium in Memory of Thomas Merton CS 3

The Eleventh-century Background of Cîteaux by Bede Lackner CS 8

Studies in Medieval Cistercian History edited by Joseph F. O'Callahan CS 13

Contemporary Community edited M. Basil Pennington CS 21

Bernard of Clairvaux: Studies Presented to Dom Jean Leclercq CS 23

William of St Thierry: The Man and His Work by J.M. Dechanet CS 10

Thomas Merton: The Man and His Work by Dennis Q. McInerny CS 27

Cistercian Sign Language by Robert Barakat CS 11

Bernard of Clairvaux and the Cistercian Spirit by Jean Leclercq CS 16

MONASTIC TEXTS AND STUDIES

The Climate of Monastic Prayer by Thomas Merton CS 1

Evagrius Ponticus: *Praktikos and Chapter on Prayer* CS 4

The Abbot in Monastic Tradition by Pierre Salmon CS 14

Why Monks? by Francois Vandenbroucke CS 17

Silence: Silence in the Rule of St Benedict by Ambrose Wathen CS 22

*The Sayings of the Desert Fathers tr Benedicta Ward CS 59

One Yet Two: Monastic Tradition East and West CS 29

*The Spirituality of Western Christendom CS 30

* available in paper